# One
# Woman

Authorised, Edited and Managed
By
Maura Dineen
&
*Coiste Chuimhneacháin Choláiste Muire*
*Pádraig Ó Callanáin, Traolach Ó Donnabháin*
*& Mícheál Ó Ríogáin*

**Copyright** © Coiste Chuimhneacháin Choláiste Muire, **2011**

First Published in Ireland, in 2011,
in co-operation with Choice Publishing,
Drogheda, County Louth, Republic of Ireland
www.choicepublishing.ie

**ISBN**: 978-1-907107-90-0

A CIP record for this title is available from the
National Library


Proofreader: Mr Joe Armstrong

Cover Design by Paddy Joe Lowney ©

# Preface

Why write a book about one good woman, Margaret Jean Dineen? I have met so many outstanding women in my life and there are many more whom I will never meet but whose lives deserve the greatest praise. Nevertheless, I feel urged to undertake this book. I wish to share with you my boundless admiration and everlasting love for this woman, who also happens to be my mother, praise the Lord.

I have been a little saddened by the knowledge that some people do not favour this publication. I have had to weigh this against the good of putting this story in the public arena. It seems to me that the life story of this person has a value that merits my doing this. So in this spirit and for the glory of God, whose work of art she is, in a special way, I offer it to all, in the hope that it will do good and that you too may be enriched and inspired by the life she lived; a life which touched the lives of many but whose inner truth was truly a life hidden with Christ in God.

# Contents

**Appendix 1**
**Appendix 2**
**Appendix 3**

# Acknowledgements

The Management team would like to thank all who contributed in any way to this publication and our hope is that you will be pleased with the final draft.

# Part I

*Margaret Jean Connaughton*

# 1 Her Youth

Margaret Jean Connaughton was born in the little village of Ballinagare, Castlerea, County Roscommon on 8 February 1912. Her parents had a two-storey house on the main street where she spent her youth, along with two sisters and nine brothers. Another sister, Delia, had died very young. They are all dead now, God be merciful to them all.

Her father, Hugh Connaughton, was very industrious. He worked hard and was happy to see people well occupied, as he understood how the devil makes work for idle hands. He had a farm and he operated sawmills, some distance from the house. He was also an occasional builder. Later on he built a beautiful house for one of his sons, Sonny, and it is still standing today and very solid. He also did some carpentry, making carts and wheels. Having nine sons in a small house, he worked out a system writing out jobs on a slate that each was to do and this was placed on the mantelpiece every day after school for each to consult. It worked very well and the boys learned how their dad meant business when work was needed.

Their mother, Mary-Anne Connaughton (née Oates) was a tall quiet-spoken woman who minded the house and the shop, which was part of the house. It was a grocery of all sorts, as shops were in those days. On the first Friday of every month, she invited all the neighbours in, who had gone to Mass, for a cup of tea after their long fast since midnight. This was done in a true spirit of Gospel love and my mother always remembered those mornings as lovely, grace-filled occasions. I have no doubt it helped to form in her that spirit of disinterested love for others and which was so characteristic of her in later life. The true neighbour is the one who does a good turn when the occasion is there and in total freedom, which doubles the love.

It seems Margaret Jean was a very lively child and one brother remembers her as always running; in contrast to her older sister, Eva, who was a placid type and loved to play the piano. There were cousins about four miles up the road and often messages went back and forth. When the children were asked to do so, Margaret Jean would always be gone ahead running. Then on one fatal day, she was running across the yard barefoot when she stood on broken glass and a deep wound resulted with much blood.

The doctor came and he tended it as best he could, telling her parents that she must stay at home from school for about one year. She would have to stay entirely in bed, with as little movement as possible, until the danger period was over. So she did but soon discovered that lying in bed, doing nothing, was so boring for someone who had been so lively. One day she heard talking outside her window and she tiptoed to the window but alas the wound opened, blood came and she was in trouble. She tried to doctor it herself; so afraid was she to let the doctor know that she had disobeyed him. She never told anyone at the time but for the rest of her life she had to live with the consequences, as the healing was never fully complete. It always gave her trouble but she was able to walk, dance and run as if it was normal.

When she was able to get up she still had to stay at home from school so she spent a lot of time in her mother's kitchen. She would see how often her mother prayed and this proved to be a very powerful influence on her whole life. She had to sit a lot of the time, so finding nothing else to do she would take up her mother's prayer books with so many prayers and she would often read them all, deepening her prayer life.

In the Connaughton home prayer was important. Sunday Mass was a must and, as many of the boys were altar boys, daily Mass was regular enough too. The sacraments of Baptism, Confession, Holy Communion and Confirmation were all observed in due order together with any devotions in the village church. The Stations of the Cross were especially esteemed. The rosary was prayed together as a family every night at a time when all could be there. The Angel Guardian was a real person and a much-loved friend.

In due course, Margaret Jean went back to school and possibly due to the long absence, she loved school and loved to do her homework. She told me how one day an inspector came and asked her class if anybody knew the Irish for Christmas and whoever did would be given a money prize. She was the only one who remembered the word *'nollaig'* so she came home with her prize money. Later she would teach Irish so maybe already as a young girl she had learned to love it.

In a home with so many brothers, she was not expected to work on the farm so she worked in the house and helped her mother to keep it clean. One brother remembered her as always washing the floor and as often giving out to them if any of the brothers dirtied it with their farm boots. Her mother cooked every day for the big family so Margaret Jean helped her and learned all the basics of cookery and laundry in that busy house. Her mother did everything quietly and well and this had a big influence on them all. Mrs Connaughton, who was very much loved by her husband and children, had charge of the shop and the three girls helped her there too.

Hugh Connaughton put a high value on a good education and it was his wish to send all the boys on to third-level and the girls to secondary school, at least. He was disappointed that, after second-level, his sons tended to want to get a job and earn money. Some emigrated to England. In the end they all did well, lived good lives and prayer was important to them. Margaret Jean showed a huge interest in books and learning and really wanted to study. Noting this, her parents decided to let her go on to third-level.

About this time Margaret Jean started to go dancing. In those days, dance halls were primitive enough. She was a good dancer and she loved it. However, her dad was strict, and didn't let her go often. She stole out a few times without her dad knowing it. The brothers knew and instinctively felt it should be stopped. Maybe they feared lest something awful befall her. So they worked out a little strategy and next time, as she was stealing back up to her room, all in darkness, she hit something and an almighty crash ensued. Her father appeared and she had to explain herself and needless to say she got a fine spanking. The brothers had so arranged several steel buckets that she would inevitably touch upon returning to her bedroom. After her dad's stern reprimand, she never did it again. This is a form of brotherly love that works well and can only be fully operative in a family rooted in the love of God. It was corrective and may have spared her some dreadful woes, but no doubt they were never applauded for being so co-operative with God's designs.

Time passed, Margaret Jean finished secondary school, and headed off to university in Dublin. She went with friends and made more friends there. She loved the social life in college, especially dancing, but she failed her first year exams. It was a heavy blow for her parents. She resolved it would never happen again, asked to be given another chance and she returned to college, never to fail again. From then on exams were important and would be given priority. In due course, she graduated with a bachelor of arts, a bachelor of commerce, and a higher diploma in education.

While at college she met her future husband at an intervarsity debate. I don't know if they kept in touch but they both ended up in teaching posts in Portlaoise: he taught in the boys' school and she taught in the girls' school.

# 2 The School is Founded

During their time in Portlaoise, Margaret Jean Connaughton and Jerry Dineen often spoke together because it was from here that they came to Clonakilty, West Cork, to set up a school. Jerry grew up in Ballingarry, County Limerick. He had two brothers and one sister. His father had a good farm and his mother Bridget had a grocery shop that sold everything, as was customary in those days. Jerry always retained a deep love for Ballingarry and the farm there and returned as often as he could.

He liked books and study and when the opportunity was offered him, he gladly went to University College Cork. He was studious and stayed with his Ryan cousins in Cork city, whose friendship he always valued and cherished. (Jerry Ryan, later Monsignor Ryan, was my godfather.)

Jerry Dineen graduated with a science degree, and a diploma in dairy science and a higher diploma in education. During his college years he used to think deeply about life and his future and a particular idea began to take root in his mind. He would provide education for poor boys in an area where it was not available so that those boys who could not afford to go to boarding school would not be deprived of secondary education. He believed in education, the kind of education which would equip people for a good job but also enable them to take their place in society in such a way that they would contribute to the betterment of society, doing good instead of evil. It was a noble thought but unless he put it into practice it would have little value. He knew this and he became more and more determined to realise this one dream of his.

He confided his project to his Cork cousins and they encouraged him, but suggested he would need a business partner in setting up a school. He agreed with them and asked them to pray that this would come about.

After some time, he informed his Cork cousins that he had found a suitable person. They were delighted and looked forward to meeting him. Imagine their surprise when he walked in with a woman; introducing her to them as his partner in his ambition to provide secondary education for poor boys. She spoke little, was very polite and so were they. However, as soon as they could speak to him alone, they told him he was foolish and that she was a hopeless choice, and that he really needed a man. He understood their reaction. Nevertheless, he insisted that she was a very good choice, that he was very pleased and there would be no man to replace her. They could see his decision was made and they left him to continue for they could not stop him. They wished them both well.

About this time, Margaret Jean got word from home that her mother was dying. She immediately went home to be with her mother. She ran once she got near home, fearing lest her mother was already dead. Still panting, Margaret Jean entered the room where her mother lay dying.

"Oh, Jean, I'm so happy," her mother said and she repeated it, but got no further.

Margaret thought she had wanted to say, 'I'm so happy to see you'.

Her mother made another attempt to talk and in one gulp said, "I'm so happy, I received Our Lord today."

This surprised and humbled Margaret Jean but it also uplifted her.

What a wonderful mother! These were her last words and her legacy to her daughter. Margaret Jean recalled the words of the Gospel: "He who eats my flesh and drinks my blood has eternal life and I will raise him up on the last day."

These words took on a whole new life for her, knowing, "His words are spirit and they are life". The faith and the love and the sincerity with which those words were said were an anointing for her and from then on her own devotion to the Blessed Eucharist was deeper and purer. God blesses the love of mother for daughter and the reciprocal love of daughter for mother was strengthened to reach similar heights.

After a short time her dear mother died. After the funeral Margaret stayed for a while with her dad until her work obliged her to leave him.

"I wish I were in the coffin with her," Hugh said, speaking volumes of the depth of his love for his wife.

An uncle told me that when he was about to get married, Hugh, his father, had told him, "If you share the bed, you share everything".

That was Hugh's faith and his respect for both God and his wife. God's way is always the best way but we must first live it, in order to discover its truth and its wisdom. Our loving, heavenly Father could only command us to do what is best. Trusting him is the key.

After the school year closed in Portlaoise, Jerry and Margaret set their sights on Clonakilty. Having researched many areas, they found it was in need of a secondary school for boys, since the nearest boys' school was in Bandon, some sixteen miles away. Clonakilty only had a secondary school for girls, run by the Sisters of Mercy.

There was much to be done: a premises had to be secured, rooms had to be converted into classrooms and everywhere had to be cleaned. They had to procure or purchase desks, blackboards, chairs, tables, presses, and books. Toilet facilities and recreation space were also needed. Both of them were children of Mary so they agreed to call it St. Mary's College, putting the new school into the care of Mary. Our Lady's role in the school was important from its foundation. She would always be hallowed and invoked there.

Jerry and Margaret Jean started from scratch but their hopes were undimmed.

# 3 School begins to Flourish
# and their Marriage

My parents came to Clonakilty in 1938 when Jean was twenty-six years old and Jerry was thirty. They started the school that September. They found reasonable premises and, having made their mission clear to the people of Clonakilty, they enrolled the few boys who came. They had basic necessities to begin with and they learned as they went along. Every teacher taught a little of the Catholic religion while daily prayer was a regular feature from the beginning. They were dedicated to the task in hand, to which many past pupils have testified. They wanted to devote all their skills and gifts to this service. Slowly but surely the school began to grow. The timetable had to be carefully worked out and the whole business of getting the school to be recognized by the Government was a priority from the start so that they could provide full state exams for each pupil and so that the teachers could be state supplemented.

The townspeople observed them as townspeople do, some sceptical or dubious, unbelieving or even hostile. Some rich people continued to send their children to boarding schools but gradually more and more country boys availed of the opportunity now within their reach. Many parents invested in the school and were eager to be part of it.

The school was four years old when Jerry and Margaret decided to get married. From the very beginning this was a likely possibility and now it came about. They married and honeymooned in Dublin in December, during the Christmas holidays. They were soon home in Clonakilty as Mr and Mrs Dineen.

During the next several years the school continued to grow and thrive. More pupils were enrolled each year and it quickly increased from a three-teacher to a five-teacher school. The input from teachers, focused on the true good of the pupils, was first-class; ever a hallmark of the school.

As numbers increased, Jerry and Margaret Jean looked for another premises. A former fever hospital, situated on a small hill, on the outskirts of the town, near the road to Inchydoney, was bought and became the final home for St. Mary's College. It had quite a bit of ground around it so it seemed to be just what was needed. It was a high building so could cater for several classrooms. It so happened that an elderly couple already inhabited the ground floor of the building but as the building was big and the new proprietors were still young, they agreed to let them remain as tenants, at a minimum cost. They never interfered with the smooth running of the school. The only problem arose, much later, when pupil numbers grew and it became necessary to ask them to leave and, as is often the case, they did not want to go.

Mr and Mrs Dineen started their own family and, between 1945 and 1951, six children were born. It was characteristic of both Margaret and Jerry to ensure that a young and growing family would not hamper, but would rather enhance, the true good of the school. And so it was that the dedication of both founders was such that there was a time for everything. The Christmas, Easter and the long summer holidays were made use of so that both school and family were fully catered for. A growing unselfishness was the only way by which this could be achieved and that was the way forward.

As scripture says, "He who loses his life for my sake will find it."

It was hard at times but the Lord helped them and they were nourished regularly by Christ's own spirit in the Eucharist. They were inspired by the original vision and with a determination to let nothing get in the way and so were able for the small daily efforts to realise it. Obstacles came and went but they were only seen in one light: they just had to be overcome.

And so the school developed and began to prosper. Both founders were excellent, dedicated and committed teachers. No stone was left unturned in their efforts to further the true good of the pupils. Religion was a subject nobody was qualified in but it was always part of the timetable. The school had to compete with other schools participating in state exams and, like any other school, it was subject to inspection by the state.

It must have often happened that Mr and Mrs Dineen were together in the evenings correcting copies. On one such occasion, Mammy was absorbed in the work when Daddy, who was beside her, suddenly knelt down to pray the 'Our Father'. Taken by surprise, Jean asked him, "Why did you do that?" His reply was even more unexpected! He said, "Oh, today I was really cross with some of the boys and I fear I may have been a bit too harsh so I am asking God to forgive me and undo any harm I may have done."

My mother said little by way of comment but this episode was never effaced from her memory and it was many years later when she related it to me. I would say it had a powerful and restraining influence on her own method of teaching, making her ever more keenly aware that all we do is done in God's divine presence.

So the years passed and all was going well until tragedy struck, as it does inevitably in every life. The cross must be faced head on and the following of Jesus with His cross must be real.

# 4 Tragedy Strikes

Jerry Dineen wasn't feeling well and this had been going on for some time so they decided to see a doctor and hopefully this would cure him. However, God's plans are not ours so in due time he was informed that he had a form of incurable leukaemia and while he could still live for more than twelve months, that would be it, unless a miracle came about.

This was devastating news for both my parents. At first, Jerry Dineen attempted to reverse the facts, as it was hard for him to believe that God really wanted him to die: he had a wife, a young family and the school! His life-project was only just on its feet, doing well, thank God, but still needing lots of work at every level and the mere thought of its having to close was unthinkable.

However, the facts were clear: he had only twelve months to live. Being a good Christian and devout Catholic he began to talk to God, to argue, discuss and even seek to persuade Him to change His mind. But God's answer was always the same. It took a long time, but eventually he was able to accept the wonderful grace of total resignation to God's holy will and he died a most peaceful, holy and happy death.

However, during those twelve months he worked unceasingly to prepare his wife, children and the school for life without him at the helm. His main focus of concern was his dear wife. Margaret Jean had a young family of six children and, when Jerry died, Emer, their youngest, was not even two years old. And the school was equally important.

It was only after considerable thought and deep prayer that he felt he knew God's mind on what should be done. He would ask his beloved wife to keep the school going on her own; until such time as someone else could manage it; and he felt she could still manage her growing family. In his mind there was no other possible solution, particularly as there was no one else able to take over the school at that time. It was a big thing to ask of his wife but he could see no other solution.

My mother was still in shock that her husband would die within months and now he was asking her to run the school too! It seemed impossible. She told him she would not be able to do so, however well-disposed she was. But he encouraged her and persuaded her that she would be able and that God would help her, if only she would trust Him more. He wrote pages and pages, advising her how to deal with the six children. He wrote in such a way that she would have guidelines right up to third-level. Sadly, my mother burned these when we got to that stage so I never got to read them. She read them and was guided by them, led by their spirit rather than being bound to each detail.

Naturally, she found it hard to accept such a huge task. It seemed impossible without him, having to manage the school and care for her family. She felt inadequate and thought it would be better if she got a job as a teacher, earning enough to rear her family. But God's will for her was becoming clearer every day as Jerry gently persuaded her, pointing out how all those boys in the school would otherwise be deprived of secondary education.

When he became so ill and weak that he could no longer teach in the school, she continued to do so on her own. This helped her to see that it was possible and, as he remained in the house for several months before he was hospitalised, he continued to encourage her towards accepting full responsibility for both school and home. She said she cried a little every day, so much so that after the funeral she rarely cried.

He had to go to hospital for the last three months of his life and she could only visit him occasionally as the Bons Secours Hospital in Cork city was thirty-three miles away and, in those days, she did not drive a car. Gradually, the real situation was becoming clear to her and all he said was sinking in. Now, as he lay dying, she was able to reassure him that she would do as he wished. She would trust God to help her day by day and she would work and live in the shadow of his memory until her task was completed. So, strengthened by this assurance, given in deep faith, he was able to fully accept God's will for him and to die with fullest resignation to God's designs, trusting and believing that they were best.

# 5 Significant Events from Childhood

I wish to record here a few significant personal memories of my dad. The first incident occurred when I was about three or four years old. Before this episode, it seems my dad often brought me and others to the school, frequently by car but sometimes walking, especially in good weather. It seems I learned the route to the school, which was relatively straight with just two corners to turn and then up the hill. It was long for a three-year-old but Dad often carried us.

One day while Dad was teaching, I asked where Daddy was and was told he was in the school. I decided to go to the school myself and find him. I walked the familiar road alone and up the hill until I came to the school door. I climbed the big steps to the first corridor when I heard his voice. However the door was closed as he was teaching a class. So I went towards the voice and knocked on the door. A sudden silence ensued until I heard, "Come in". Slowly I opened the door and all the boys' heads turned around while Daddy, at the far end of the room, was looking anxiously at the door, thinking it might be an inspector, but they saw no one, until my eyes, looking past all the boys, lighted on my father and I uttered the one word: "Daddy". All the boys looked down now and saw me, a little three- or four-year-old girl. Everybody laughed and Daddy picked me up to bring me home.

My Dad must have meant an awful lot to me if I could do that on my own!

That incident is better understood when seen in relation to the next incident which proved to be much more significant. I must have been four or five years old. My father was still in our home in 16 Emmet Square, but was no longer going to the school and spent most of the day in bed upstairs. My Mother, my brothers and I were in the kitchen, having our breakfast before going to school. Mammy said to me, "Eat your porridge". I said, "No." Again, Mammy said, "Eat your porridge or I'll slap you." My reply was, "I'll slap you back". Instantly, the three boys said, "We're telling Daddy." In vain did Mammy try to prevent them, saying, "Don't upset Daddy, no don't go." But they were gone like lightning. Soon they were back with the command to me, "Daddy wants you." I was trapped. All I knew was I had to go up to Daddy. So I left the kitchen and started up the stairs, with my back to the wall, slowly but surely, step by step. I arrived at Daddy's bedroom and he saw me at the door and said, "Come over here." So, still holding up the wall, I moved slowly towards him and just when I got right beside him, he put out his hand and hit me across the face.

It wasn't an almighty blow as it did not knock me but it stung me and I was deeply hurt so I turned away from him and I looked for a place where I could go and sit down and hate him for evermore. I was about to do this when he put out his hand, in a gesture of friendship and said, "Let us be friends again." For a second or more, I hesitated and then, before I could make any decision on the matter, the Almighty and all-powerful power of God intervened and it was as if God Himself took out that little hard heart of mine, now turned to stone, and He replaced it with a much better one so that I became filled with love and forgiveness. I found myself overflowing with love as my heart sang and I took his hand, overjoyed that, yes, we could be friends again. This was a profound moment of merciful love that could only have come about by God's power.

It was years later that I was able to interpret this incident in that way. His whole being was upset for my mother's sake. He knew what she had to face and to think that I was going to be a brat, on top of everything, was too much. So his parental love and authority enabled him to slap me in such a way that the slap was ministered in a true spirit of parental love and correction so that it had the power to call forth the power of God's grace and merciful love on me, at that instant, in full measure. The impact of that grace was such that I never forgot the incident, nor did the effect of its grace ever leave me. It was thus I learned that forgiveness is God's gift and the truth of Alexander Pope's words, "To err is human, to forgive divine." As adults, we can choose to forgive or not but the power to actually do so belongs to God and, since He died for us, it is something He will never refuse. But we must want it and ask and pray for it.

One final incident occurred while he was in the hospital. It was sometime during the last three months of his life. My mother and two or three of the boys and I were in to visit Daddy. It seems it was our last visit though I was not aware that I would never see Daddy again. My mother sat on a chair beside him, while we stood around. There was a priest in the next bed and he called me over to give me some chocolate he held in his hand. Mammy said to go over and I did. He shook hands with me and the chocolate was in his hand. He held my hand and I could not release mine. I felt the chocolate was melting and I was wondering how I could tell him but no words would come from my mouth. Then I looked closely at him and it seemed to me I saw Jesus living in Him. A powerful sense of the presence of God came over me and enveloped me, a glow of warmth and love and it all seemed to be coming directly from this priest, from God dwelling in him. Surely it was Jesus, alive in him and He was manifesting Himself to me! Could it be my dad had confided to him his fears, lest we would be a trouble to Mammy and maybe he asked that priest to pray for us and me, and to bless us and me? It was a wonderful blessing. Then he released my hand and sure enough the chocolate had melted and I went back to Mammy and gave it to her to throw away. But I felt so happy and I had a great love for that priest.

There was one other patient in the ward, a layman, and I could see he had grapes. He called me over but I did not sense the presence of Jesus in him as I had in the priest and neither did I fancy grapes so I was reluctant to go to him but Mammy urged me to go so I went and I took the grapes he handed to me and as I did I felt he lacked that beautiful sense of love the other man had. Somehow, I felt that by going to him, I was able to give him a little of what the priest had given to me. Having come back to Daddy's bedside, Mammy told us all to say goodbye. I hoped we would be back soon but we never returned.

The nurses brought us down on the lift. It was my first ever experience of a lift and it was a fitting end to a beautiful experience, which had been like getting a lift to Heaven for a while. Was God telling me in this lovely way that my dad would be carried to Heaven just like that and it would be a happy flight! Surely if that was what I experienced in that sick hospital room, God must have been there in a wonderful way.

Later on in my life, my mother told me that many priests used to visit that Dominican priest in the bed beside my father and they would all bless Daddy. Then, on one of those visits, a priest asked him if he would like to become a Dominican tertiary as it would bring him many graces, especially now being so close to death. So he said he would think about it. Some time later he gave him his answer. "Father," he said, "God has said that 'in my Father's House there are many mansions'. Well, when I die I hope to be in the same mansion as my wife". It was thus he declined his offer but only on God's terms. All the above speaks to me of the deep and true faith my father had, which entirely governed his life and his thinking. Many years later I asked my mother if she would like to become a Carmelite tertiary and she recalled to me the above episode. Her reply was, "No, I will stay as I am." I suspect she was hoping to be in the same mansion as her husband!

# 6 Jerry Dies but Life must go on

So it happened that on 16 May, 1953, Jeremiah J. Dineen was laid to rest. He was well prepared and so was his dear wife Margaret Jean. The whole of Clonakilty was aware of his death and of the fate of his widow with six young children. As yet they were unaware of how she would cope. The whole of Emmet Square was filled with people on the day of the funeral. Although I was only five, I can remember people everywhere on that day and our big house was full of strangers. We, the six of us, spent the day with our good neighbours who kindly gave us our meals. Then it was decided that I should go to my relatives in Limerick for a while. I was very pleased and remember going back home to get my new shoes. I noticed Mammy kneeling upstairs in tears. She told me to go with Aunty Mary and I said I would. Soon afterwards I was in a car with my aunt and uncle on our way to Daddy's hometown, Ballingarry. I stayed there while Mammy tried to get to grips with life without Jerry.

The funeral over, my mother decided to go back to school the very next day! She did this because the Intermediate and Leaving Certificate exams were only round the corner and she felt she could not let the boys down. For her, it was necessary. Besides, as she said herself, she had done all her crying for months and from now on did not need to shed tears. A brand new car was delivered to my mother's door soon after the funeral, with instructions from her deceased husband that she was to learn to drive, as this would be a great help to her. She said otherwise she would never have considered it as she felt she had enough to do without having to learn to drive as well. However she set about learning to drive. Her instructor was Mr Murphy, Western Garage, Western Road. She did learn but, truth to tell, she was never considered a good driver. Too nervous, she preferred to drive slowly and hated overtaking cars. That said, she drove for the next forty years. She drove to school and, over the years, she did this thousands of times. Had she walked each time it would have made her teaching career far more difficult. Later on, she found it a real blessing as it helped her to be independent. She often drove to Cork city. When we were in primary school she would often bring us after school by car to Inchydoney, a local seaside resort, for a swim and then back in time for supper.

During his last years, Daddy had encouraged her to smoke as he felt it would help her to cope better. She did this at his bidding but, like all habits, it was difficult to stop. While she was a moderate smoker most of her life, she indulged in no luxuries. In fact, her lifestyle was austere and she enjoyed simple things for recreation.

When the state exams were over, this year of her husband's sad death, Margaret Jean was in the classroom while some of the boys were preparing to go home for the summer holidays. As she watched them, it suddenly hit her full force that while most of these would return in September, Jerry never would. September after September flashed before her mind's eye and they seemed to be endless as she saw herself returning each year without him. The raw reality of it all struck her as never before. All the pent-up sorrow she had suppressed found release as the tears began to flow and as she said herself she could not stop them.

The boys watched in awkward silence, wondering what to do. Gradually she became conscious of their presence and their embarrassment so she tried to pull herself together and it was then, in that precious moment, she began to minister to them. Through her tears she said, "Well, boys, as we go through life we all meet the cross and we all have a cross to carry but if we can accept the cross He sends us, taking it from His hands, and if we trust Him, it will all work out."

Then she became calm again but her definitive *'fiat'* had been given. In place of the dear husband she had lost, she accepted this new family of school children along with her own young family of six, from His divine hands. Was it not similar to the exchange Mary, her mother experienced on taking John as her child, when Jesus was taken from her on the cross? Despite her broken heart, she was assuring them of God's goodness and faithfulness to those who trust Him.

For her it was as yet only the beginning. It was what she wanted to believe and do and, for the next thirty years, it was possible for all to witness that she did just that as she faithfully carried out the mission entrusted to her. Her fidelity to her dead husband's dying wish was to guide her for the rest of her life. From that time on Margaret Jean's trust was in God and, despite being severely tested, it never wavered until she reached the end of her journey.

The transition for me was much simpler. My mum and dad had been so solicitous about every detail that my life was little affected. The love my dad had for me was such that it simply continued, though the dad I now had was my Father in Heaven. He was invisible but I had total confidence in His love for me. My mother's love was always there for me and as the years passed I understood this better and better.

# 7 Daily and Yearly Chores

Quickly her life developed an overall pattern that never changed in major ways over many years. However, within that there were many changes but above all life was lived to the full. Needless to say, for many years, the school meant nothing to us and so we were no help to her at all. She had accepted this would be so and never upbraided us for this. Rather, she sought in countless ways to ensure that our childhood was as happy and carefree as she could make it.

She rose early every school day in order to prepare breakfast for our family of six and herself. At this early hour she often baked a loaf of brown bread for the evening meal. As the family were still young she had to get us ready for school. In fact, for a couple of years two of the girls were too young to go to school. I have vivid memories of her combing and plaiting my hair, finding clothes or books we needed, even lacing our shoes, finding raincoats, and filling our lunch-boxes, although these were very basic as my pals always had nicer lunches. She helped us with all these little things even though her own needs were much greater. However she always seemed to be totally attentive to us although we knew, deep down, that she had a busy schedule but children can be so selfish.

We usually had a simple breakfast together in our small kitchen and each one did one's own wash-up and then we all got ready for school. If it was pouring rain in the winter she would often drive us to school first so that we would not get too wet and then proceed to her own school. She had to open the school so she had to be there early. This meant she could not attend daily Mass as it was too much of a rush to have breakfast at 8.30 a.m. However, come Lent and Advent she would always try to do that and rarely missed doing so while her good example greatly encouraged us to do likewise. One result was I loved going to daily Mass and still do.

She would spend the entire day in the school, from 8.30 until 5 p.m. As it was a boys' school, I was never a pupil there so I had very little first-hand knowledge of Mrs Dineen, the teacher. While in national school we would be home about 3 p.m.; later in secondary school it would be 4 p.m. She usually employed a girl to clean the house and to cook dinner for us. So on arriving home from school we would be expected to eat our dinner and could play around until Mammy came home. Her arrival was always a happy event and I loved to know she was in the house. She usually had copies to correct and business to do. She would usually inform us of what she had to do but supper was soon ready and we always ate it together and she would listen to the news on the radio afterwards at 6.30 p.m. Mostly we would linger on at the table and have a laugh together and this was a time when one of my brothers would have us all laughing.

The time after supper was meant to be study time although it was never rigidly enforced. We all had homework to do and so had Mammy so we simply got on with it. As Mammy worked hard, a strong work ethic prevailed in the house so it was normal to work and to study well and, while some were more studious than others, we all enjoyed study. Often we would go to the dining room, which had a very large table and do our work there in her presence. It was there we would often find her fast asleep on the chair beside the fireplace. She was exhausted and sleep would overcome her. However she would soon wake up and get busy with whatever she had to do and she was never idle. As she had so much schoolwork to attend to herself, she never bothered to examine us unless we actually asked her to help us. I found she was so good at Irish that it didn't pay to ask her much as she seemed to discover all I did not know very quickly. Generally she trusted the nuns who were teaching us to take care of that. The family rosary was said about this time and was rarely missed.

At approximately 9.30 p.m. she would finish and her ritual was to go to the kitchen for a hot cup of milk and a biscuit while she made the porridge and then off to bed. She would say she was tired and had to go to bed and she hoped we would go soon too or as soon as we were ready. We often stayed on until 'top of the pops' played our favourite tune and then we would make for bed. We were slow going to bed but slower getting up. However her example of regularity was a beneficial lesson, as finding it hard to get up we knew we should have gone to bed earlier.

Holiday times were different. As she was teaching and we were at school our holidays were mostly the same, Christmas, Easter and summer holidays. The lead-up to Christmas was very exciting for us as kids. Santa was so real to us and as she was such a good mother, she provided the Santa gifts each year in such a way that believing was easy. In hindsight, I think it must not have been at all easy for her to do this, yet she assisted us in every way, helping us write to Santa and getting to know what we wanted in order to get it in good time as she had to do it all herself. She purchased everything and more, and hid them so well we never found them until Christmas morning at the foot of our beds. Then we all went to Mass joyfully on Christmas morning and on returning home spent the day playing while she cooked the turkey dinner along with the plum pudding and Christmas cake which she had made well in advance. As she prophesied herself at the time of Dad's death, 'Nothing will be neglected'. Then the graces of Christmas and all the gifts given with such unselfish love combined to make the rest of the Christmas holidays a very happy time. Needless to say it was always spent at home.

The Easter holidays were short. The first part, Holy Week, Holy Thursday to Easter Sunday, were spent mostly in church. She would not have missed these grace-filled days for anything. Her determination was enough for the rest of us to follow suit. We followed her lead, happy and carefree, as the precious gift of herself to God was re-enforced at this time. She saw the church as her second home and told me often that one of her deepest wishes was to be always near a church. So an influence like that deeply affected us and me in particular. The next week flew as exams were looming and the pressure was on and the time was short so we made the most of it.

The summer holidays were different. She always wanted us to have a real holiday so it was a regular thing for us to go to Ballingarry, County Limerick (my dad's home) for the summer. My brothers stayed with Uncle Patrick, the farmer, while the girls stayed with Aunty Mary who had a shop. It was all so different and we loved it. Besides our Uncle and Aunt were very good to us and did all they could to make us happy. My mother would often drive us down but she would return alone, driving that long journey on her own. Sometimes we went on the bus. She rarely had a holiday, as she was very glad of the summer holidays to work on the school. As we got a little older, she was very anxious to send us to the Gaeltacht during the summer, so we went there often and loved it. So, too, love of the Irish language, music and dancing grew within us. She would make all the arrangements and would help us to pack, giving us all we needed and so we went with glad hearts. It was a big adventure for us and she never dampened our spirits. While we were away from home she kept in touch and would write to us regularly. She would collect us and it was always lovely to be going home again with her. Later she encouraged us to go to France to improve our French and to get to know the culture, or to Germany if that was one of our subjects. She was very broad-minded and considered it educational to travel, especially when young, although she was always careful to make sure necessary precautions were there and she had great trust in us.

The school had to be cleaned and she had to do it. Bit-by-bit she would work on it. Once back from our holidays we would often go to the school with her. I saw her scrub wooden floors and it would leave her exhausted. She would do a little each day so that she could cover a large area. Besides there was no alternative; She told me once that she did ask a woman to help her but when her work was done she told her, 'Never again.' So to avoid any gossip my mother decided to simply do it herself. The old wooden stairs in the school were steep and there were many of them and these also had to be scrubbed.

We would often be with her as she worked but she did all the hard work. Her sense of respect for us was such that she would not burden us, as this was her work and not ours. We were oblivious of all she was doing so when she did not press us we did precious little; sweeping, yes, but that was it. So she continued in this heroic way for many years, never consciously thinking she was heroic because it was all part of her gift of herself to God.

It was backbreaking work but I can still see her heavenly smile when she would call me to say proudly, "I got all that much done today, I'm so pleased." I would look at it and compared to the size of the room it was indeed a small area and despite all the hard work in never looked like new but noting it was still wet I would say, 'Yes, that is done all right.' That was all the praise she got but she was not depending on human applause but was driven by something much deeper. The consolation she reached out for was just her humanity whispering, 'I can't do anymore today but at least it is something.'

The walls had to be distempered so she would get my brothers to help her, especially the higher parts, but she also had to do some and to oversee it all, buying paints and brushes, and then the clean-up! The toilets had to be cleaned and for years she did them herself. This weekly chore would see her wash out the stone floor in a jiffy with a deck-scrub and I can still smell the Jeyes Fluid. If I mentioned that it was smelly she would laugh and say, "It's gone now." She was always for cleanliness. Every Friday evening she would try to sweep the classrooms and I would help her as I liked sweeping floors but these were not easily done. A few times she tackled the big windows and I tried to help her but it was hard going. There was a sort of air about the place and a sense of freedom, a place where good things were done and where goodness presided in a special way. The school was on a small hill so the air was fresh there and it had a simplicity and a beauty all its own. She would often say, 'I'm going to the school, would you like to come?' I liked to go with her.

Maybe it was all a part of her and I sensed this! In spite of all she did, she never laid burdens on others. She would never ask us to do anything that was in the least degree unreasonable to ask but for her there were no limits. She was committed to doing all in her power so that everything would be well done and nothing would be neglected

Keeping the building safe was another big chore. The school was an old and very high building, built on high ground, so the winters were very cold and often stormy and slates were liable to fall off and would have to be replaced. A complete new roof would have been ideal but it was so expensive. However she did repair whole portions of the roof when this had to be done. I have vivid memories of stormy winters when she would face out to school, never thinking of how cold it was or how cold she would be that day or how cold others might find it but fearing lest more slates would fall and the rainwater would be pouring in. Happily God did not let it happen but the fear was always there and it was so real. Many times she thanked Our Lady of Fatima, (whose picture she was pleased to have in the school) and the green scapular, which she always kept there, for saving the boys from serious accidents.

The desks and chairs had to be mended, or replaced as the case may be, so carpentry skills were frequently required and she got to know some good carpenters. She often went to local auctions to see if any bargains were available and I can still see her joy when she found them. She also looked for nice furniture for our house at 16 Emmet Square in this way. She really wanted to keep the house looking well and over the years she kept improving it.

The remainder of the summer holidays were spent at home and as most of the cleaning was done at this stage she would concentrate on getting the books in order for the next school year. This meant trips to Cork city bookshops and occasionally to Dublin for schoolbooks and school equipment. She never consulted us but had it all worked out herself and would know exactly what to order. The books would arrive by post or courier and would be sent straight up to the school. She developed a system over the years whereby she would arrange for some boys to sell the books to the other boys and the sale of second-hand books was always a big part of this commerce. The lads enjoyed it and I got the impression that Mammy enjoyed it just as much, especially as it was a big help to her and she trusted the boys to do it well.

Her main concern was that the books needed would be there and that none would be lacking. This must have been a big job in itself but for her it was one among so many others. She did not have a proper filing system or cabinets although she hoped to one day, but it never happened. However, at one stage she installed a small library for the school with lovely shelving and books and was pleased to have done this.

For many years she had to supply books for every subject so she had to consult other teachers to know exactly what was needed. She did this very well, helped no doubt by her own reverence for books, which she passed on to us. As well as books she had to keep supplies like chalk, pens, pencils ink, biros and dusters.

As her commitment was total, she soldiered on, never looking back, never questioning all she had to do. Her life took on a basic pattern which was constantly changing, yet always the same, and within that everything else took place; all the ups and downs of life, all the important events of life, all the growing up from one stage to another took place in and around this yearly cycle of events, depending always on God the Father, who was watching over her and whom she trusted.

# 8 How she Coped

In this chapter, I hope to pick out events and happenings that occurred over the many years of our growing up that help to highlight the quiet heroism and genuine charity of this noble woman who lived to fulfil God's holy will for her.

I recall an episode from my childhood which was of great significance for me. I must have been about eight or nine years old and I was in bed at the recovery stage after some minor illness and I was reading a story from a large fairy tale book. I was reading *Snow White and Rose Red* and I had just made the discovery that all the stories in the book ended with the words, 'and they all lived happily ever after'. Mammy came into the room to visit me after her day's work at school. She asked me if I would like her to read me the story I had open and I said, 'Yes.' So she read it to me and as it was not very long she soon came to the words, 'and they lived happily ever after'. So I sat up and asked her, "But did they really live happily ever after?" "Yes," she said and rose up from the bed with a far away look in her eyes while I was fully focused on those clear blue eyes of hers. Then she continued, "Oh, yes, they did, all of them, they lived happily ever after."

She had moved to the door and was gone. But during those few seconds the action of grace was indeed powerful. Her spirit of charity won while, for a brief instant and surprised by my question, she struggled with the very different reality of her own story and her concern for me that it was not the moment to dampen my hope that the fairy tales were true. My eyes had been riveted on hers, God managed to bond us, mother and daughter, in a special way so that from then on I was always careful to seek to please the inner spirit of my mother and not just the letter of what she might say to me. For me it proved to be a powerful moment and it showed me how the love of mother and daughter (or son) is always under the scrutiny of the Almighty as He seeks to pour out His blessings, wherever He finds no obstacles.

It seems to me that God was pleased with my mother who wanted her child to have a happier life than she had. Thus God was able to bless me bringing our relationship to a deeper level. This became a great grace in my life as, bonded so deeply to her, I was empowered much later to avoid many pitfalls that could have been disastrous but instead was guided from within to better pastures. This taught me anew the value of seeking to do all things well.

Thanks to my mother's strong spirit of dedication to God and her growth in unselfishness over the years, my childhood, spent under her loving care, was very happy. Despite the fact that she had to be mother and father to us and run a school, she was determined not to deprive us of our childhood and all the joys and sorrows of a normal upbringing.

In those days, the sacraments of First Holy Communion and Confirmation were big occasions for us children and we looked forward to them. My mother was never actually free to attend these ceremonies as she was teaching so she did what she could. She prepared us as any mother would, showing huge interest in all the details of dress and whatever was needed and as always was most generous in this regard, wanting whatever was required. Then she would arrange for us to go to her old friend, Mrs Murphy, for the day and she would take care of us like any mother would until my mother would join us later in the day and bring us home. They were special days and my mother kept them special for each of us.

Saint Patrick's day was another big holiday in our local town and for weeks everybody seemed to be involved in preparing for the Saint Patrick's Day concert. All the national schools used to participate, the girls did Irish dancing and singing and drama, the boys did wonderful singing in Irish, while the grown-ups would put on excellent drama and sketches. A lot of organisation was involved and this was provided voluntarily by many of the people of the town. All in all it was a great day and most enjoyable. There would be lots of children doing the Irish dancing so we always got doing something, usually part of a six-hand reel or whatever. So like the stars of the show we had lots of practices and the nuns were so helpful wanting us all to do well. Then the day came and there would be two shows, one in the afternoon and one at night so that everybody got a chance to see it. My mother could never go to the matinee but she would run down to the later show and usually leave the moment it was over as she had to be ready for school the next day. All we wanted was for her to see us and she would say she did and we were fine, and then we would have a great chat about the whole show for a long time after that. In a similar way she was ready to participate at any event where her presence was in some way required but the school always came first. We understood this and knew it had to be so.

Her spirit of work was simply there. We never questioned it but it formed us so that for me work was a normal part of living. The biblical teaching that it is according to the dignity of man to work was easy to grasp. Like other children, I often wished I could stay in bed and not go to school and not have to do lessons or practise the piano and I often wasted time but living with someone who worked unstintingly as she did was to become a huge inspiration to me in later years and the longer I live the more it influences me.

I always loved to be where she was except when she was cross and giving out and this did happen sometimes. For many years my mother's school was open for five and a half days. This meant that she went to school every day for six days a week and the one day she was free was a Sunday. There was enormous pressure on her to continually master herself and to go up to that school, hail, rain or snow, and to be there early to open it and remain there all day as Principal and Manager until she closed it in the evening when it was empty.

Sunday arrived and we went to Mass with her. After Mass and Holy Communion we would have breakfast. Then she would start to give out to us, usually about nothing in the sense that there was no just cause.

Whatever it was it always seemed silly and of little consequence but she went on and on and I hated to hear her as she seemed to lose control of her tongue. Then gradually she would calm down and say no more.

Later she would cook the dinner and spend the rest of the evening correcting copies. There would often be a quick trip to the school. We usually had evening devotions in the local church in those days and this was always a pleasant duty. We were never forced to go but her eagerness to be there was our main incentive. She then prepared the supper for us all, made final preparations for school next day and it was bed time.

The point I wish to make here is that her body and spirit could not easily adapt to the freedom of a Sunday, especially so as Monday would soon follow. So it seemed to me that in order to adapt herself to the absolute luxury of no pressures as were involved in being mainly responsible for the huge building, full of teachers and pupils and where the work ethic was really high, God, whom she had received in Holy Communion, came to her aid by letting her let off steam, in our presence until such time as, humbled and relieved, she would be able to relax. She would even apologize later, after a fashion. She seemed to know she should not have said what she said but to see her happy and relaxed was a great reward.

This happened again and again and I never held it against her, as instinctively I knew it was a sort of necessity. I knew she would stop and be sorry, as this was the pattern. She was simply trying to relax but she was not able until such time as she managed to inform her whole system, body, soul, mind and spirit that it was okay to relax now. However it was only for just one day as on Mondays the working week would begin again. So it was quite an achievement, as she had no guru or professional in psychological or motivational science to instruct her on the way to deal with this. She simply had to rely on her own common sense and need at the time. It woke me up to all she had to cope with alone and caused me to admire her great inner strength that was so determined to keep doing what was laid out for her to do.

Mammy smoked most of her long life. Cigarettes helped to calm her nerves while she was actually smoking but they had a way of aggravating them also so it was a mixed blessing. She did try to give them up from time to time but was generally unsuccessful and besides she was never a really heavy smoker. Her spirit of self-control was always in supreme command. She had a policy whereby she never wanted the boys at school to actually see her smoking so this meant very little smoking at school and she usually relaxed with a cigarette on returning home. In my opinion she had no other bad habits.

I would like to highlight some significant episodes that occurred at school. I always recall my mother telling me never to leave a teaching post in the middle of the year. Aside from the fact that you are breaking your original contract with the school, it has detrimental effects on others. In her situation it created many problems. For many years, Mammy had only enough teachers for the classes that she had and if one teacher was absent for a day it meant somebody else had to take their classes as well as their own. This was not easy as some classrooms were upstairs and others downstairs and, besides, the burden would often fall on Mammy, being the one in charge. So for a teacher to leave his job during the school year was to create a trying situation, especially for Mammy. I must say that this rarely happened. There was one particular situation which I remember very well.

One teacher was offered a job nearer his hometown and truth to tell he had been hoping this would happen for some time and Mammy was aware of this. However the fact that the offer came in the middle of the school year was a blow and as he feared losing the new position entirely if he did not accept it immediately, she decided to let him go without upsetting him too much. On returning home from school that day Mammy was very upset. She explained the situation to us and we understood but, as teenagers, we felt helpless to do anything about it. So we went through the motions of supper together and the usual chores but a gloomy air prevailed. How we wished we could do something but it seemed impossible. Then at about 7 p.m. on this dark winter's night I saw Mammy put on her coat and I asked her where she was going? "I'm going over to the church," she said. That was all. My instinctive answer was, 'A lot of good that is going to do,' but noting that she wanted to go and knowing there was nothing to be gained by staying in the house, I said nothing, thinking within myself, 'Well, if that helps you in any way, good luck to you but it would not be my way of dealing with the problem.' So she went off on her own and we remained where we were, still rather silent. After some time she came back and to my amazement, her attitude seemed totally different. She was bright and almost cheerful. As I had been pondering despondently over the whole situation, I was taken aback and I blurted out, "Did you get a teacher?" She turned to me and said, "How could I get a teacher. I went over to the church to pray about it. I'm going to put an advertisement in the paper as soon as I can and just hope for the best. There is nothing else I can do."

I was flabbergasted. The woman who went out and the woman who came back were so different. I began to wonder why and in my childish way I had to admit that she had been visibly comforted and consoled in some strange way. She had only been to the church so God really did help her. This really puzzled me and I never forgot it. Years later I understood this much better. It was in ways like that that she handed on the gift of faith to us and certainly to me. The witness she gave was so powerful and real. Suffice to say she did get a teacher soon after but at first she was a bit sceptical, saying, 'He is probably hopeless and could not get a job anywhere else but if he is anyway okay I will take him on as I have no choice.' And so she did and he was far better than she expected and remained for a few years. The moral is that when God helps us He really does help us.

From the very beginning of the school, provision was made for outdoor games and the boys were encouraged to play them. Once the school moved up the hill there was more room and the Clonakilty playing pitch was nearby and the boys were allowed to use it. Later on more formal inter-schools games were organised and the boys did well in them. An indoor ball-alley was also part of the school on the hill from the beginning so the lads would have somewhere to go on wet days. As time went by they developed their own football and hurling teams under the name of St. Mary's College. Mammy liked to appoint one teacher to oversee the games and to help the boys organise matches. This worked fine and there was always a teacher interested enough to do this. However it sometimes happened that a match would be due and the sports teacher would not be free to go, for instance if he was away that weekend. So it used to sometimes fall to Mammy to accompany the boys on the bus to the match, as she did not want them to go without some supervision. She had no wish to go for herself but it was the only solution on several occasions. In fact some of the lads thought she liked to go. On meeting her once having returned from a match, I said to her, "Who won the match?"

She said, "Oh, we lost."

I said, "Oh, what a pity."

She said, "Thank God, no more matches for the year." I was a bit taken aback and then she added, "I didn't tell the lads that, they were so disappointed."

She did introduce some elements which might never have come about had she not had such a hands-on experience of the matches. She noticed that at half time the boys wanted a drink and were in need of something but just had to manage as best they could. So she decided to bring along a quantity of oranges and at the halftime break each player was given one and I have no doubt but that this was a big help to them. She also noted that they were all in different jerseys so she decided how much nicer it would be if they were all dressed the same and it could be more evident that they were all playing for St. Mary's College. So she duly purchased jerseys for the entire team, black with white collar and cuffs. This was a time when jerseys were rarely seen. She also got the boys to contribute a little to the cost and she gave her share. They were only used for matches and when not in use they were kept in our house. They usually had to be dried out and cleaned but were rarely washed. The boys were very pleased with this and no doubt it helped them to play even better. In fact the jerseys were so admired that occasionally when the local technical school had a big match, they asked to borrow them. She gladly lent them.

# 9 Things she had to Manage

She had many victories over herself and she simply kept going to reach the heights of God's will for her. I compare it to the mighty 'fiat' of Mary. She learned to come closer to Mary as she very humbly asked Mary to help her carry her cross and she knew that because of Jesus and Mary she would never walk alone. It was her great faith which would carry her through. In fact, she once told me that Daddy sometimes said to her, "You are the second woman in my life." I was taken aback as I enquired how she could accept that! She explained that Mary was the first and she was the second. He had also told her the she most reminded him of Mary. Truth to tell I did not fully appreciate those sentiments at that time, thinking to myself that I would like my husband to put me first or at least on the same level as Mary. However, later on I understood better and how lucky I would be if my husband had a similar devotion to Our Blessed Mother.

The school grounds were spacious but not enormous. There was a large playground surrounding two sides of the school building, while a third side belonged to the ground floor tenants, the other side was a small grassy area. Fields bordered the schoolyard area and most of it was leased or rented to neighbours for grazing cattle. The boys would sit around and eat their lunches and snacks there. In general it was quite spacious and adequate. There was no traffic so it was generally peaceful and for them alone. It commanded quite a view looking down on Clonakilty Bay. I'm sure Mrs Dineen kept a watchful eye so that the place was generally litter free. Mostly it was used at lunch break or whenever there might be free time between classes. I understood that most of the teachers went elsewhere for lunchtime, such as to their homes or lodgings or to a restaurant, but it was the custom for Mammy to remain in the school building all day until she closed it in the evenings.

She would take her lunch alone in the building, mostly glad of a little quiet time to get herself together and prepare for the afternoon. For many years her lunch consisted of a bottle of milk and a banana and one cigarette, unseen by pupils. Sometimes she might have to go to the yard for one reason or another and would invariably meet some of the pupils. As she was the Irish teacher she always spoke to them in Irish. This practice came from a deep desire not to miss any opportunity to up their Irish skills but also to further maintain discipline, which was always necessary and to do so in a non-threatening and mature manner.

She always spoke clearly and distinctly. She once confided to me that, as a lot of her pupils were country boys, they did not always speak clearly or well and that a stranger would find their accents difficult to understand. Besides she knew that many of them would end up going to England for work and she felt people there might not know what they were saying and some would make fun of them. So she tried to help them in this way by always speaking clearly and well. She never remarked on their accents or humiliated them in front of other boys who spoke better. She simply gave the good example and hoped it would benefit them. In this her method was *noblesse oblige*.

The part of the building facing the town had a large field bordering it which was the property of the school and as the years passed she had a strong desire to improve its appearance by getting a row of evergreen trees planted there. She did buy small plants and hoped they would root well and grow into sturdy trees that would look really nice near the school. The first lot failed so she got professional advice and service but for some reason they never grew really well. She did try several times and in the end decided to leave it. Some trees did eventually take root but nothing to what her hopes had been.

Much closer to the school there was a small grassy area so she planned to put a large hedge there to beautify it somewhat. She wanted to keep the grassy area but by adding the feature of a nice large hedge hoped it would help hide the bareness of the building in that corner. This too was professionally worked on and to her delight this hedge grew well and flourished. I thought it was a fine hedge and she would often point it out to me saying, 'It is doing well so far and thank God it improves that part of the building.'

Once planted all of these had to be minded and grass cut and mowed, hedges clipped and weeds kept at bay. It wasn't very difficult but there was no one else except her to tend to such things. As I said, we were not much help to her.

She never seemed to look back at all but kept following her star and relied on God to provide whatever rest, recreation or uplift she might need. Her way seemed to be just one way and there was no room for hesitation. The school was very demanding at times but with her total dedication all fell into place.

However at one stage her health was run down a bit so she had to go to the doctor for a check-up and he warned her that she must have a midday meal so from then on her lunch was sent up to her three days a week. One of the pupils would collect it from our house and give it to her.

All of her hard work was hugely formative for her. She learned to transcend herself more and more so that her spirit grew strong in God. I can still see her turning the corner of the square of houses where we lived and walking resolutely straight home. I was beginning to admire her and to consider within myself, 'How does she do it?' I sought to analyse her but I could not. Scripture came to my aid which says, 'The spiritual man judges all things but he is judged by no one.'

Once I was sick and went to bed and when she arrived home after a long day at work she made her way up to my bedroom and I was so touched by her genuine concern. She assured me that I could stay in bed the following day also if I needed it. I was amazed as I was not very ill, just out of sorts; and the quality of her totally unselfish consideration for me was like balm. I so wanted to be like her on that day.

# 10 The Work of Teaching

My mother often said that while she loved teaching she did not like managing a school. She would have loved to teach and then be finished. The general opinion seems to be that she was, by all accounts, an excellent teacher. She was a natural communicator and so her ability to impart knowledge was both natural and professional. She explained to me how some pupils were naturally quick and intelligent and would pick things up easily and well, while others were naturally slower and found difficulty in learning. So she devised her own methods and one was that if she was teaching something for the first time she would explain it to the whole class to the best of her ability, using the aid of the blackboard if required and then she would repeat this teaching a second time and even a third time if it was particularly hard to grasp. Then when she felt it was well explained she would ask a very bright lad to explain it and after him another clever boy and only then would she ask a boy who was not so smart as by now he would have heard it four or five times and would be able to answer reasonably well. It seems this method worked well for her. If a boy was slow or behind the others she would take him aside and coach him individually after class, and often after a long day at school herself. She was prepared to do this until he caught up.

There was always a place for humour during her teaching, as intense learning sessions often erupted into moments of laughter, enjoyed by the whole class, especially herself.

She was very thorough. Her own subjects, mainly Irish and commerce, were thoroughly mastered by her and her communication of them was equally good.

During all these years while she was teaching she had the wonderful support of a great friend who was also a Christian Brother, who taught Irish in Synge Street, Dublin. He helped her considerably whenever she had any questions about the on-going teaching of Irish. He also became a good friend to her children as he liked to remember each of us on our birthdays. He visited us occasionally so we met him and it seemed to me he was much older that my mother. Eventually he died and was missed by her and by us. May he rest in peace.

My mother kept records meticulously. Roll-books had to be written up and kept updated; although this was one of the easier jobs. Bursar work and stamps of all kinds, involving both herself and her teachers, had to be understood and worked out properly. She did all this and kept abreast of everything that needed to be done. At times I would see her filling in various forms and official documents and she would labour at such things and concentrate until they were completed. I would consider that she got very little credit for all she had to do. Later I began to understand those oft-quoted words, 'Virtue is its own reward.' It was all part of her total dedication and fidelity to her deceased husband's dying wish, that she would keep the school going as long as God wanted it.

The bank was another chore she had to attend to. She believed in lodging most of her money in the bank. She never spent much on herself, keeping to a frugal lifestyle. She saved whatever she could in the local bank, mostly for our future education. When the time came she sent us all to college. She was never in debt and right up to her eighty-sixth year she managed her own bank account, and as soon as a bill came, she would write the cheque so that it was paid immediately. She was in every way the enemy of any form of procrastination. She was very generous and, while growing up we seemed to live on a tight budget but once we moved to third-level she would supply us with whatever we needed and was careful to include a generous amount of pocket money so that we could cope well while away from home those first few years. She was kind to the poor and I remember her collecting our old clothes and shoes for a local beggar woman who had lots of children. She would sometimes refer to her own mother who was so kind and good, especially to the poor.

My mother was good to the missions and we used to get a lot of the missionary magazines. The Cork mission to Peru was a special case. She gave publicly to this cause but she also supported it privately. I remember one particular evening we made a visit to the church together and I saw her put some money in the 'support Peru' moneybox. She told me the Bishop had asked at Mass that the people should support it. Out of curiosity I asked her how much she had put in and she said thirty pounds, which would be about €200 today. Nobody but myself knew of this action and I was very edified by it.

As a family we were never short of necessities but there was no extravagance. We enjoyed a little treat now and again. On our birthdays she was not always able to make a cake but we were always warmly greeted on such occasions and this meant a lot to us. Her spirit of generosity grew with the years and must have had its effect on the school also as she made that journey from being partially redeemed to being fully redeemed. In so far as it was required of her she made herself available to all and her care of others was always a reaching out from the heart and she did all she could to help and assist others. She had first-hand knowledge of God's care for her; she knew all the hairs of her head were counted, and she gave herself more and more to Him.

As I said before, Mammy loved to receive Our Divine Lord in the Eucharist but she was also very faithful to the sacrament of reconciliation and generally gave us every encouragement to avail of it also, though she rarely had time to check up on us. One particular day she came home after having received this sacrament and she was radiant. She told me she was walking on air and when I asked, 'Why?' she told me the priest who had heard her confession had said to her, "God loves you, not the lady next door or down the street but you." I said that I thought she knew that and she agreed but insisted that it was the way he said it that made her feel totally loved by God in a way she had not felt before . I was surprised so she ended up saying, 'He probably said the same to everyone.' But she was still wonderfully uplifted.

For most of the life of her school there was no staffroom. The only place for teachers to meet and leave books was in the corridors that, although large, were neither private nor warm. My guess is that all staff meetings or encounters with individual members of staff must have taken place there or in classrooms that happened to be empty. Classrooms were also scarce, four in all, but at one stage she divided one large classroom so she did have five rooms after that.

She often wished she had better flooring, especially when she was washing them. Eventually she improved some but it was only a little at a time. Trying to get workmen was not easy and time was always limited, as she never wanted workmen there while school was in progress. At a much later stage she got a science laboratory built. It included provision for a teachers' staffroom. This gave her great satisfaction as it was a bit like a dream coming true.

While her main subjects were Irish, commerce and religious instruction, at times she also had to teach other subjects. In those days one had to pass Irish or fail state exams. This was really serious so she had that added responsibility. To the best of my knowledge she was the only ever Irish teacher in the school. She loved the Irish language and knew her subject well and over the years perfected her knowledge of it by keeping abreast of how Irish was taught at the time. She was always very much attuned to exam papers and kept herself up to date with curricular requirements in all subjects but especially in Irish and commerce. She rarely spoke Irish at home but we sometimes said the rosary in Irish. It seems her grasp of Irish grammar was second to none and so too her appreciation of Irish culture was deep and loyal. She was not musical but liked Irish music and dancing. For years she taught *Peig Sayers* and this was a favourite with her. I often helped her to sort old schoolbooks like *Seadhna* and *Cúrsaí an Lae*. No textbook was ever discarded but were treasured and used until it was beyond repair. She had a reverence for books, which she passed on to me.

My mother was very good at teaching commerce and pupils rarely failed. In fact honours and high honours were the norm for her pupils. She was decidedly exam-oriented, as she knew this would be the crucial decider. However she was not only focused on exams. She wanted her pupils to be good citizens, people who could take their place in society in such a way as to help build a better country for all. Hence her role in career guidance began. Having taught a class of boys for five years she could see that once the Leaving Cert was over those boys would leave the school forever. Having loved them for five years, working solely for their good and proper welfare they had, in a sense, become family to her so, always true to the high ideals which had brought the school into existence and the even higher ones which had motivated her to continue its existence single-handedly for some thirty years, she looked on each successive Leaving Cert class with the eyes of a truly good teacher, guide and friend to the young. As far as she could, she would take each pupil aside at some stage and ask them what they planned to do after their Leaving Cert.

In a friendly but disinterested way she wanted to know if they had plans for a particular job or what work they had in mind. Some boys would have their minds made up and if she approved of their decision she would quite simply praise and encourage them. Many would not be so sure so, drawing on her wisdom and experience, she might suggest something that might be helpful in their particular case or perhaps enlighten them on some point of which they might be unaware. If a boy had no plans whatever she would tell him clearly that that was not the way to end his five years of education at her school. It was important that he should be at least considering what sort of work he would choose and what sort of job he would like to do for the rest of his life. She urged and encouraged him to have some job in view unless, of course, he wished to further his education by going on to third-level. If he still failed to suggest anything, she would them summon all her acquired knowledge of him and his character over the previous five years and give a very practical suggestion as to what she thought might suit him. Sometimes, her suggestion would be accepted while at other times he would agree to think about it but at times her ideas would be resisted. There would still be time to meet him before he left school so she did what she could while she could before she would spiritually and lovingly send him on his way into the world, happy now that she had done all she could and confident that God would take over from then on since her time with this individual was up. Just as on that 16 May, 1953, she had handed her beloved husband over to God, a pattern was set whereby each pupil of hers, having finished his course, was in like manner handed over to God's care, while she continued her work with the others whom God gave her. For her, God was always the giver. She accepted each one as from His hands, not mystically but actually because the extent of her reverence and respect for each one could only find explanation in such an exchange.

I remember one September when Mammy was preparing for the first years to sit for their entrance exam and the thought came to me that it must be hard for her to say goodbye to the Leaving Cert class, having journeyed with them for five years and the fact was she might never see them again. Surely the thought of having to start all over again with a new set of boys was a bit tiresome! I remember her coming home this particular evening, after a new set of first year boys had completed this entrance exam, and I asked her how it went. I was amazed at her response. "Oh", she said, "they are just lovely. Seventeen boys came. I can't wait to start teaching them, they are so nice". Her enthusiasm just bowled me over. My own thoughts, as expressed above, were totally at variance with this burst of energy whereby she committed herself instantly and totally to their education for the next five years. Much later I understood it was all part of the charism, whereby, led by God, she seemed to receive directly from Him all she needed to continue her work with that total dedication so characteristic of her.

# 11 The Exams

Exam results were very important to her, though for her it was never just a matter of brains. It was the persistent, hard and persevering honest work that went into the years before the exams that really counted with her and she always encouraged the boys to adopt this spirit, insofar as she could inculcate it into them. She always made it very clear that she much preferred a worker to pass his exams than someone who had brains but who tried to avoid the hard work that would have perfected those brains. Nevertheless, when all was said and done, the exams had the final say and she wanted her pupils to leave her school with all the qualifications necessary to secure a job or to further their education. In practical terms this meant a good Leaving Cert.

She worked really hard to get the boys through their exams. Even in this she relied very much on God, having a particular love for that prayer which included these words, 'Grant us, Lord that we be asked only those questions that we know,' as one past pupil told me. Seeing how well she did her part I have no doubt but that the good Lord was almost obliged to answer this plea seeing that it was for the benefit of others. I do remember a Protestant boy coming to her school with almost no knowledge of Irish and so she arranged to take him for extra tuition. Thanks to her unselfish help, over a long period, he did pass his Irish and she was so pleased. Then there was another boy who was very poor at Irish and she offered to help him privately as she did not want to embarrass him in front of the other boys so he often came to our home to be helped. She worked patiently with him right up to the exams and he also passed.

At exam time she was anxious to read the exam paper of her own subjects. Usually she would know then who would pass or who would not. Mostly she was right. She always liked to be there when the boys emerged from exam rooms to quiz them a bit and to make sure if her own assessment was okay. Her main concern at this stage was the borderline cases; who would pass or fail and those who might attain honours or just miss it. Later in the summer the results would come. By the time I became aware of the significance of this day for her, she would already have survived several years' results. I remember her telling me she rarely had failures in Irish or commerce. Subsequently I noticed how very well most pupils did in these two subjects. Religion was never an exam subject in those days.

I have very vivid memories of results day. The post usually arrived at our house between 8 a.m. and 8.30 a.m. On results day, always during the summer holidays, she would wake up and, before dressing herself, she would hurry down to the hall door and come back up to the bedroom with the results in her hands. She would very carefully open the large envelope and spread it out on the still unmade bed. She took no notice of me watching her, except that she would speak out loud from time to time, in this way acknowledging my presence. She would scan the results and get the overall picture. They were usually as she had predicted, although at times there were surprises. The failures, if any, were always foreknown, although she eternally hoped for a scrape through. Then she would scan them again in more detail and names of boys would be mentioned while saying he got this or he got that. It went on for about a half-hour, after which she would dress herself and bring the results downstairs to be examined properly saying, "Thank God the results are okay." I would say to her, "I'll go down now and get your breakfast." She would murmur a faint, 'Yes,' but, like a magnet, her eyes were back on the results sheet.

It was all absorbing for me as I sensed that other world she belonged to so totally and I wondered again about it. I knew it was her job and she earned her money in this way. Yet somehow it was so much more than just a job. While it was a job that was very demanding in the sense that she had many things to attend to there, it was also something far more for her. She was totally dedicated to it and to doing it well, yet without her family ever feeling we were neglected because of it. In fact I think we benefited hugely because of her absolute commitment to offering it the highest standards of which she was capable. So I too was irresistibly drawn into the dynamism of her charisma.

In a sense we were her main confidants. Although we were young, for many years there were no others for her as she sensed it was more discreet to act thus as most other people in the surrounding area were potential candidates for her school or she was connected with them in some way. It seems she needed us just to be there, to share in some small way the ups and downs of her position. I waited until she felt she was sufficiently informed so as to be able to dress herself and have breakfast before she could make a further study of the results. At this stage her mood would be set, usually contented, despite a few disappointments here and there, but there were no major catastrophes which was a relief.

The next task was that the results had to be sent to the regional West Cork newspaper, the *Southern Star*. So as soon as she could she would draft this. It was always a straightforward piece with the overall results. It was the custom for most schools to do this in those days so she felt likewise obliged. If the results were good it was good publicity for the school but if not so good then she would try to make it look good without altering the facts. As the school was fully recognized by the Government she was entitled to promote the school in this way.

The next stage was telling the individual boys their individual results. The procedure was that the results were only to be given to the individual boys themselves and they were required to call to our house to collect them. It sometimes happened that other family members might phone or make enquiries about results but we were instructed to say that the boy himself should call for them and if this was not possible Mammy would speak to the person making the query. Usually the boys preferred to call and normally it was not inconvenient to do so. So if I answered the door on that day more than likely it would be a pupil looking for his results. I duly motioned him into our parlour having asked him his name and I would tell Mammy the name so she would go and speak to him with his particular results in her hand.

She had each boy's results written out on a results sheet with full details. I remember her being really well dressed for the occasion and she would go with a beautiful smile on her face. Then, after a visit of about fifteen minutes, she would return radiant saying, 'He was very pleased and, yes, he will go on for whatever had been his choice. I have given him the details he needs and he is anxious to get started.'

I remember too the odd exception when a boy had failed. Maybe he was not very bright or he had worked a bit but not enough. So she would be a little sorry for him but not too much as she had already decided what was the best thing for him to do and would advise him so that he would not wallow in self pity for long. I used to take a note of the names of any who failed so that, should I meet them at the door, I would be sensitive to what they would have to face.

Such a boy would also be sent into the best room so, when I told her, she would hastily pick up his papers and march in. There would be no words of condemnation or anger as this too was part of the job. I wondered how she would deal with this type of situation, as he would already know that many of his classmates had been successful. Once I just caught her opening words before she closed the door as follows, "Well, did you think you would pass?"

In this way he knew immediately and the worst was over. So she stayed with him as long as the others or maybe longer, if necessary. Then she would return and I would ask her how he took it. "Well, he knew he couldn't get it." Or she might say: "I advised him to try again but no he won't. His brother has work and he will work for him. He may be as well off as he was never inclined to study."

Of course each case was different but her attitude was wise and caring and she did all she could to direct them to whatever she thought was best. When a boy failed she was sad too but the old saying, 'It's no use crying over spilt milk,' was her style. The Inter Cert results were not quite so important but bad results there were used as an incentive to work harder for the Leaving Cert and especially so in fifth year. She used to tell the boys, 'What you do in fifth year will be a big factor in what your Leaving results will be.'

Apart from exams, the school had a high standard of excellence and this found particular expression when the entire school had occasion to rejoice when four of its pupils raced to victory in an all-Ireland debating competition in 1979. They achieved the honour of being first in Ireland, putting St. Mary's College in the limelight on a national level. This was no small achievement as a total of 318 schools took part and altogether 226 local, 37 regional and seven national level debates took place. It was the first time a boys' school reached the final and, in addition to the team award, Raymond O'Donovan, one of the team, took the individual speaker award. The competition was organised by the Junior Chamber, Ireland, and the Educational Building Society. The entire school shared in the joy of the occasion and indeed the whole of Clonakilty as in one way or another everybody was someway involved. Mammy was very happy too.

# 12 The Future of the School

It was thus the school developed and grew and managed to achieve a degree of excellence. The exam results were always good. Past pupils mostly found good jobs and lived good lives. Many had very happy memories of their time at school and most criticisms could be put down to Mrs Dineen's own standards of austerity and which she unthinkingly placed on others or due to her high regard for her pupils whose good she seemed to pursue at all times first and foremost.

As the years passed so too the number of pupils increased. Then one day Mammy realised that she could do with the ground floor of the school building for extra classrooms. As it was still occupied, she did a little research and discovered that the couple who lived in the school also owned a house property in the town though they had it rented to a family. She decided to ask them if they would consider leaving the school as she needed extra room. She really felt they would as they were both quite elderly and she felt the steep hill up to the school was too much for them. However, having been so long there they were reluctant to leave at all, insisting that the hill was no trouble and the air at the school was good for their general health. Mammy really needed the extra space so she pursued the matter further and was obliged to visit the family who occupied the house in the town. They were also reluctant to leave their house although alternative accommodation was possible to get. I was with her on that occasion.

The only alternative left now was to go to court and this was the very last thing she wanted to do but she had no other option. She went to her solicitor and explained the situation to him and he agreed to take on the case and assured her that things would work in her favour but she would have to be prepared to give compensation as this would simplify the whole procedure. A date was set and that day came soon enough so she asked me to go to the court with her. It was my first time in court so it was a big experience for me. Her solicitor had told her to say very little and he would sign to her when she should say anything. She did exactly as he told her because it was all very traumatic for her. She agreed to pay compensation and she won the case. As soon as the ground floor was vacated, she set about making it into classrooms and decided to get lovely new floors there. She was very pleased with them and, as she said herself, 'They are a gift to wash.' It was a case of 'all's well that ends well' as both families got new homes and they were happy once they settled in.

However her time for managing the school was coming to an end. Her age was already beyond the usual age for retirement so she was looking to the future of the school. None of her children seemed to want to carry it on. One brother, Donal, taught in the school with her for one year but subsequently found a post elsewhere more suited to his degree. One of the girls, Eithne, worked in the school with Mammy for several years and was with her at this crucial time. Mammy did not encourage us to continue the life of the school as she wisely felt its day was over, as community schools were fast becoming the schools of the future; a trend she did not try to reverse, although she was aware that they too had their shortcomings.

For many years previous to this she had entered into negotiations with the Headmaster of the local technical school about merging her school with his to form a new Community College for Clonakilty. These talks continued over a number of years and she attended all necessary meetings so that she would be fully informed of what would eventually be decided. Her main concerns seemed to be that the new school, as an Institute of Secondary Education, would continue to provide that service for the people of Clonakilty; that all her pupils would be entitled to transfer to this new school without any difficulty; and that all her staff would be assured security of employment in this new school, if they so wished. All of these requirements were duly met and she herself was offered a teaching post in it also but she declined this offer on the grounds that she could now retire gracefully as she feared that having been a manager for so long she might not be able to be as good a teacher to a new manager as she would like to be.

The negotiations for this project took several years and a new building was erected for the purpose but eventually it materialized as satisfactorily as she had hoped so that, when the new Community College opened in 1980, no one was as happy as she was. In 2011, that Community College still serves the people of Clonakilty and helps to carry on that ethos of providing a good education for the people there today.

# 13 Retirement

Some people in Clonakilty were aware that Mrs Dineen was about to retire and wanted to acknowledge the wonderful work she had carried on for the benefit of the people of the town for her entire adult life. She was nominated as a recipient of the Festival of West Cork Hall of Fame Award. In fact, she had been offered it some years previously but she declined it on the grounds that she was still teaching and so her work was not yet complete. Now, she was conscious that her work was done and that it would be appropriate to accept it. So she said, "Yes," to the people who offered it but she mentioned this forthcoming tribute to nobody, least of all to us, her own children.

She knew it was a public tribute but in keeping with her usual lifestyle, she thought she would be able to get it over with as little fuss as possible. It was only by chance and a mere day or two before the event took place that some of us heard about it. In fact, if my memory serves me well, we probably asked politely who would be the recipient that year and on being told it was to be our mother, we quickly questioned her to verify the facts or even to inform her as she did not seem to know. However, on questioning her we realised to our amazement that she was fully aware that she was the one and had already decided what she was going to wear. "So what's the fuss," she asked! I was really edified and amazed at such simplicity and humility. Of course this was in keeping with her entire philosophy of life, which always sought first to please God knowing that all these other things were his gifts anyway. Besides, she was deeply conscious that she could not have done it without Him and if she could transfer the award to Him instead of her, she would have gladly done so. But this time, He was insisting that her part of the work should be praised and acknowledged.

I wondered how she could cope with retirement. She, who had been so very active for so many years, was now reduced to doing very little. Her health was good and she was still a very active person so I urged her to take that job in the new school but to no avail, as she had decided that this was not for her. She even mentioned not wanting to deprive a young teacher of a good job. So I just hoped things would work out for her and they did.

She settled into her new role with admirable dignity. At this stage, both of my sisters were married with children and, as one sister was still quite near her, she became a wonderful babysitter when required. This bonded her with her grandchildren in a wonderful way and I could see how grandparents have a wonderful role to play. She did the same for the other grandchildren but as they were far away she did what she could. The love and respect she had for them used to delight me and often in those days when she came to visit me she would be full of stories about them, mostly amusing, and we had some delightful conversations about them in those days. Having such wonderful faith herself, she sought to instil in them some of that faith, which was such a mighty support in her own life. So according as she had opportunity, she would bring them to church for a little visit, pointing out Jesus and Mary, saying prayers with them and giving them holy water.

She was so childlike herself that she was very much at home and at peace with the youngest of them. She always had a sense of humour and this found scope as she played with them and lovingly watched over them. She once confided to me that she had wondered what God wanted her to do after she retired and she declared with admirable submission that her place was helping to mind the children.

However, my sister later moved to settle in County Kerry and so there were times when no children were with her. Her strong faith showed itself as she tried to be always at daily Mass and at any other church devotions that were available. She sometimes remarked to me that there were less now than before and she missed them. She loved the rosary and often said many rosaries a day. I used to supply her with rosaries and she would often say how she lost one. She had one beside her bed and one in her bag and in most of her pockets. I was delighted to supply her as she was always very generous to my community and I used to wonder what she would like and her only need seemed to be for a rosary beads. So her prayer life grew and grew.

She was always a people person and, although she hated gossip, she loved a chat and she had a few regular friends whom she loved to meet. Some past pupils and past teachers would come and go from time to time and she always loved to meet them and to hear how they were. It gave her the greatest joy to know that they were doing well. She took a certain pride in this but it was the pride of a spiritual mother for the sons she loved more in the spirit than in the flesh. It was also a sign that her hard work was bearing fruit but she always saw it as the combined work of Jerry and herself. She never saw it otherwise despite being so many years on her own because for her he was always there, albeit in the spirit.

So her retirement was never the problem we had envisaged. She coped equally well with it as she had coped so well with the active life when it was required.

# 14 The Bronze Plaque

The past pupils played a big role in the life of Mrs Dineen. St. Mary's Past Pupils' Union was formed in 1958 and ever since then it played an increasingly important role in her school and personal life. From the start, past pupils hosted an annual dinner dance on Saint Stephen's Day, 26 December, where past pupils were invited to be present with Mrs Dineen as honoured guest. It was also an opportunity to fundraise for the union as they became involved in many worthy projects. To the best of my memory she never missed attending this function. She was always expected to say a few words to the assembly so it was a regular thing for her to prepare a little speech. This was no small thing in her eyes and she went to a lot of trouble to have her 'few words' very well prepared. She liked to commend the past pupils for their various services, for example, awarding a silver and gold medal for achieving first place in the Intermediate and Leaving Certificates. Money was set aside for boys who wished to become priests and from time to time a series of public lectures were arranged for the benefit and on-going formation of laypeople in the town. She might also give a little account of how the school was progressing and would highlight the special achievement of a past pupil who had excelled in some sphere. One of her greatest joys was to see them doing well in any way.

The past pupils, for their part, made every effort to ensure the dinner would be first-class, while the venue was always carefully chosen to provide for the particular needs of the evening. It was always well attended, ending with a little music and dancing, so Mammy got a chance to dance again. She was happy to dance on those evenings but rarely did so otherwise.

In later years, there were class reunions and they always invited Mrs Dineen to be with them. It was usually possible for her to do so, having been given good advance notice. She always prepared herself well for these functions so that, when the time came, she was at her best. Such occasions were important to her and she seemed very aware that she was also representing her late husband. His dream for this school was always with her and she was untiring in promoting it in every way.

Celebrations marked the closure of the school, Mrs Dineen's retirement, and the fiftieth and sixtieth anniversaries of the foundation of the school. I will confine myself here to one such celebration.

The school had been closed for some years and Mrs Dineen was almost eighty years of age. The past pupils contemplated organising a function, mainly to honour her 80th birthday. Jerry Beechinor, foremost among the past pupils, confided this idea to me but I dissuaded him, as I knew my mother would be miserable if she thought the whole town knew her age. It was one thing to know it without saying it but to make it so public would never be her way. She never wanted us to mention her age; so her birthdays came and went and we wished her a happy birthday but her age was never up for discussion. Of course we knew it and it was possible to find out but it was not important to us either. So Jerry, good, kind and understanding man that he was, agreed to defer it for a while. So when she was closer to eighty-five years old, he decided to go ahead and her age would not even be mentioned.

This was a really big affair. Huge efforts were put into preparing it. It would begin with a Mass, concelebrated by two past pupils, Fr. Jim Duggan CSSp and Fr. John Kingston CSSp. Mrs Dineen would do the first reading and her son, Donal, would do the second reading. The Gospel was to be the good Samaritan and the homily would focus on how Mrs Dineen was indeed a good Samaritan for so many. Then all would proceed to the original site of the school, when it first opened in Clonakilty, now a hardware shop owned by the Sheehy family on Astna Square, and happily run by a past pupil who was more than happy to accommodate the proceedings.

It was decided to erect a bronze plaque to honour the founders of secondary education for boys in Clonakilty. Some was to be written in Irish and a rough draft was shown to Mrs Dineen to see if she was happy with it. Of course, typical schoolteacher and first-class Irish teacher, she found several mistakes and was not slow to point them out. Jerry Beechinor himself told me that she brought him back fifty years and he felt like a schoolboy again as she explained exactly and precisely the inaccuracies in the grammar. It seems she waited for the local library to open the following day to verify if she was correct. It was never her way to impose her knowledge on others; it always had to be according to the book. When all was checked out it was found that she was indeed most accurate. So all was duly corrected and sent to be engraved in bronze. Later on I spoke to Mammy and chided her for correcting a grown man. She showed complete astonishment saying, 'I couldn't have people looking at those mistakes forever and much better than having to take it down again to correct them.' I had to admit she was perfectly right.

This bronze plaque was already in place with a veil covering it and the plan was for Fr. Jim Duggan to bless it and for Mrs Dineen to witness the unveiling of the plaque and at that point she was invited to give a little speech. She had told me this and I had said how I would love to read the speech also. Imagine my disappointment when she later informed me, "someone is going to write it out for me but I will say it." I tried to impress on her that it was her sentiments the people wanted and not anyone else's but she replied with absolute confidence, 'Oh, he will write it as if I wrote it.' She was very pleased with what he wrote, telling me it really was as if she had written it. I was still disappointed but must admit that when I heard it eventually I realised she was right. After that the programme was for everybody to go to Dunmore Hotel.

Here, a big surprise awaited her as she was greeted with a fanfare of trumpets. Next she was led into a crowded hall to a sort of raised platform with a chair where she was invited to sit. It had been arranged for many past teachers and past pupils to come and greet her on this very platform. They were also encouraged to say a few words if they wished and especially to wish her a happy retirement. This was followed by a dinner, singsong and dance. The whole event was a marvellous success and enjoyed by all, and it was recorded on video and DVD.

Needless to say it took Mammy some time to recover from all this and, while she clearly saw it was a wonderful tribute both to herself and to the school, she was happy that it was all over as she found such big functions very demanding. She would rally to the occasion and, being the kind of person she was, her input always involved a major giving of herself so that the receiving of tributes was matched by that characteristic wholeheartedness whereby she never saw herself as the only recipient but rather that she was the one chosen to receive the tributes on behalf of so many others; past pupils, past teachers, husband Jerry and family, and all who had contributed to the building up of the school in any way over the forty-two years of its existence.

# 15 The Fall

She had chosen to live in Clonakilty, at 16 Emmet Square, although she was well in her eighties and her daughter Eithne wanted her to live with her in Killarney. Besides, she was still very sprightly and was happy to go to Killarney from time to time but in Clonakilty different members of the family would visit her from time to time. She was very aware that she was a great age and her time in this world was limited. She was happy in herself and she loved to pray, especially the rosary. She was delighted to be so near the church and was a daily Mass-goer and daily communicant. She made new friends among the daily attendees. She retained her great devotion to the Stations of the Cross and could often be found meditating on these as she moved slowly and meditatively from one station to the next in our big church of the Immaculate Conception in Clonakilty. As she often passed the church on her way to the shops, post-office or just out for a walk, her preference was to pay a little visit to Jesus, her friend, but as this was not always possible, she would devoutly bless herself, acknowledging his presence in this way and also her form of a wordless excuse that she would not be staying longer this time.

One of her lady friends used to work for meals-on-wheels and asked my mother if she wished to avail of this service. She declined, saying it would be wasteful to give her a dinner as they were far too big for her and she preferred just to make a little for herself. Then, the inevitable happened, voluntary staff for meals-on-wheels would go low and help was needed so the same friend was obliged to ask her if she could help and she did. The result was she began to go there from time to time but when I quizzed her on what she did her reply was, 'I do very little. K. does all the work. She gives me a few simple jobs to do but she is happy just to have me there.'

About this time too, the parish priest started a pastoral course in the parish and everybody in the town was invited to join the group. It would involve attending one or two meetings every month for the length of a school year. Imagine my surprise when Mammy told me she had signed up and had been to the first meeting. Needless to say she was the oldest member. It seems they had discussions but she was happy just to listen. I urged her to participate as I felt her wisdom would be such a help but she was not so inclined. She was happy that they excused her and she enjoyed listening and learning, as her basic attitude was essentially childlike.

She continued to read quite a lot, as she had always been a good reader. She came to know and love Saint Thérèse of Lisieux, the Little Flower, and was very well informed of her doctrine of spiritual childhood and always tried to live by it in her own quiet way.

Mammy loved to take a walk in Emmet Square and in the town as she enjoyed meeting people and especially past pupils. We used to ring each other every week at this stage as this was allowed for me. Prior to this she was always my most regular and unfailing correspondent by letter. As she was often on her own, I had the idea that she would enjoy making a little weekend retreat and besides her meals would all be made for her. She agreed to give it a try. So I made the necessary arrangements. The retreat was to be in the Benedictine Priory in Cobh, County Cork. I also arranged for a nun friend of ours from Presentation Convent, Midleton, to meet her off the bus in Cork city and both would proceed to Cobh and spend the weekend there together.

On that very morning, as I was going about my duties, I received an anxious phone call from Sr. Ursula to say that Mammy had not been on the bus or the next one. We both wondered if she had missed the bus but this did not seem to be the case. So I rang our house where she lived but got no answer. I became quite alarmed at this stage so decided to ring the local convent where I had some nun friends and see if they could check the house for us. They were most helpful and as a local priest, who knew both Mammy and myself, was with them, he jumped to the rescue. He offered to go to 16 Emmet Square immediately in his car to check the house. He knocked at the door but there was no answer so after two or three knocks made his way in to the house. There was no sign of Mrs Dineen downstairs so he investigated upstairs, searching every room but she was not in any of them. He decided to go out the back. It had rained quite a lot that morning so when he looked out the backdoor he found her lying on the concrete ground and unconscious, if not worse. He sought gently to move her but was unable so he went for help and within a short time she was brought into the sitting room and a fire was lit there. As the heat came into her body again she began to revive and clearly she was very weak but thankfully was very much alive. The doctor was called and my sister in County Kerry was alerted. It was decided that she should attend Casualty Department in Cork Hospital. My sister, Eithne, who had come all the way from Killarney, now took over and decided to stay with her until the doctors in Cork decided that she was okay and in no real danger. This was a big job as Mammy was very weak and not able to walk. My sister told me that her time in casualty, where she waited and waited and was sent from one place to another continually, was a real crucifixion for Mammy due to the state she was in. However, eventually she was free to go and they had found nothing wrong. It sounded good but she was still very weak. My sister brought her to her own house where she gave her every care and attention until she was back to her old self again.

The evening before she was to catch the bus for the retreat in Cobh, she had gone out to the back yard for some reason and she fell. Then, to her horror, she found she could not get up. She tried many times but it proved impossible for her. So judging her situation and knowing the night was before her she decided to try to make for the little outdoor toilet in the yard. It seemed the nearest place to go and she would have a roof over her head and hopefully she would eventually be able to walk back to the house. So on her hands and knees she crawled to the little house across cobbled stones and God only knows what bits of glass, sticks or nettles may have been along her path. Once in the little toilet house, she found herself so exhausted that she fell asleep. She told me the Mass bell in the nearby church woke her up in the morning so she did not find the night long. However she found herself still unable to stand up properly and walk back to the house but decided it must be done. Using up every ounce of her energy, she half-crawled, moved, pushed and stumbled towards the house. It began to rain and then she slipped and laid there in the middle of the yard, with the rain pouring down on her until some hours later Fr. O'Donovan found her. It was a mighty ordeal, which she survived, but it took its toll on her.

# 16 After the Fall

It was now clear that her walk was impaired. The hope was that it would come back but when it did it was evident that she had a foot problem. It was then she told us that it could be traced right back to her childhood, when she fell that fatal day on broken glass in the yard.

From this time on she could only walk with difficulty. Often she had to consent to use a stick or link an arm or two. Like so many others she rejected all suggestions of a wheelchair and only accepted a stick because she could not reasonably refuse it. Eventually she was able to return to her own house in Clonakilty, which pleased her very much. However the family could see that she needed extra help so it was decided to look for some home help to keep the house clean and maybe cook a meal or two for her. We were so happy to find Mrs Marian Santry and they both got on very well. Marian did the needful for her while Mammy had no shortage of cleaning jobs for her as, house-proud as ever, she wanted her house well-kept, especially as the family came from time to time and even more often now.

The family worked out a rota so that some or other of us was almost always there. My brother, Traolach, lived in the house so he was a regular but we could not leave it all to him. I asked and was given permission to stay with her for a month, which I did about eight months before she died. At that stage she no longer went to Mass every day as it took too much out of her. She would stay in bed longer now and would spend most of the day in the kitchen and on sunny days could walk in the back yard. Occasionally, my brother would drive us both to Inchydoney where the fresh sea air was healthy. She ate little but liked her three meals. She had also developed a liking for television and wanted it loud as she had become somewhat deaf. She would watch the news and also the soaps but I found that whenever I asked her about a programme she had it forgotten. I concluded she did not follow the programme but liked the buzz of it while her mind was elsewhere.

She never went to bed without saying the rosary. When I suggested she get the Anointing of the Sick, explaining to her that it would help her, she agreed and wanted it. So we arranged for it to be done and a local priest came to the house. She made her confession and was anointed and this made her very happy.

Meanwhile, the past pupils had been busy, especially Jerry Lyons. They were planning another 'do' in her honour, the sixtieth anniversary of the school. They hoped to have it in the local hotel near my mother, to make it easy for her to attend. It was to be in the month of June so I was back in Mount Carmel when she told me. Knowing her condition and how difficult she found it to walk and what slight interest she had in most things, I was sure she would decline. Imagine my surprise when she announced to me, "Of course, I will go. It is only across the road and Traolach will bring me over and back."

Needless to say, I was delighted and looked forward to hearing all about it. So in due course it came about. I was speaking to her on the phone the evening before and found her in great form and eagerly looking forward to it. In fact she suddenly sounded twenty years younger, which I could not quite understand, until it hit me that this was in connection with St. Mary's College and was all part of the charism God had given her. When anything in connection with the good of the school was concerned, she was divinely inspired and enabled to participate in whatever way was required. Her whole body, mind, soul and personality was completely at the service of what was now taking place in connection with the school, even though the school was no longer there. It was now part of the history of the town and of Mrs Dineen's own personal history. It would go to the grave with her and indeed beyond it, God bless her.

The sixtieth anniversary of St. Mary's was commemorated in June 1998. She joined several past pupils who came to Emmet Hotel for this occasion. All the past pupils, young and old, were delighted to see her. They realised she was hard of hearing and arranged for each past pupil present to have a few words with her on her own. She was delighted with this and told me later that she knew them all, even though some of them had to remind her of their names. She told me it had been a most enjoyable evening. Later, the *Southern Star* newspaper printed a picture of her in the midst of the past pupils present on that memorable day. However, when she sent a copy of it to me, I got a shock and all I could think was, 'My mother is dying,' and about seven months later she was dead, God rest her valiant soul.

Sometime after this 60th anniversary celebration, my brother, Sean, informed me that Mammy was once again going to daily Mass. I could hardly believe it but it was true. She seemed to have new energy, who knows but maybe her desire to attend Mass was so great that God gave her the strength to do it. From then until the following January she attended Sunday Mass always and daily Mass often. However her health was deteriorating and her age was against her. Her habit of smoking was not in her favour. While she never smoked really heavily, and did give it up from time to time, the bad habit was with her to the end.

In January 1999, she went once again to stay with my sister in Kerry but she was not long there when she fell in the sitting room. The fall was soft but her hip was impaired; or perhaps the hip broke and then she fell. In any case she was rushed to Tralee Hospital and given every possible care and attention. Dr. Coffey, my brother-in-law, was watching over everything and nothing happened there without his knowing it.

# 17 Her Time had Come to Leave this World

The big question was if she would survive an operation on her hip. The doctor attending her simply said, 'If it was my own mother I would do it'. So with this assurance it was decided to let him go ahead. However, he cautioned, 'First of all we must build her up as she is not ready for an operation as she is.' So they proceeded to do that and it was then we knew her time had come and God was indeed calling her to Himself. The more they tried to build her up, the more she went down. It was soon clear that there would be no operation and it was highly likely that she would soon die.

At this crucial stage, I was alerted to come if I wished to see her still alive. Because of my great desire to see her, I was given permission to go and I went as quickly as I could. I made for Tralee Hospital, but alas, she was already dead. This time, I was invited to go to the morgue to see her remains. It seems the family had just gone so I was alone. Imagine my surprise when instead of crying I found myself rejoicing as I witnessed the peace on her countenance. That dear face, always in life so harassed and worked-up except when she smiled her lovely smile, now exuded only peacefulness. I knew she was with the God of peace after her life's work, so generously done and offered first and always to God. I prayed beside her for a little while and we talked again. I said goodbye but we were not parting. My whole being was full of her and the perfume of her life would refresh, restore and delight me all my days, thanks to Jesus, Mary and Saint Joseph.

When she was in her eighty-seventh year I asked her to write her memoirs, even offering to write them if she would dictate them to me. She said she could not do it, even going so far as to say it was the hardest thing I could ask her to do. Still I pleaded with her and she agreed to think about it. So I waited, hoping she would agree to it. However she came to me a few days later and said, "I can't do it, someone else will have to do it." I noted that she did not say it was not worth doing. I hoped someone would do it but some ten years after her death I realised that if I did not do it, perhaps nobody would, so, lest I too die, I wanted to write this account of one woman, fully alive and for the glory of God.

Circa 1924. Back row: Winnie O'Hara, Mary J. Flanagan (Mrs Byron), Sadie Kelly, Irene McDonagh, Noti Donoghue, Lena Donoghue, Molly Donoghue, Mary Brennan, Delia Brennan, Jane Egan, Mrs Cahill. 4th row: Rebecca Gough, Kate Flanagan, Lizzie McCormack, Patricia McDonagh, Bina Kelly, Mary Scott, Ciss Elwood, Martha Donoghue, Annie Cunniffe, Mai Hanly. 3rd row: Bridie Noone, —, Eileen Brennan, Mary J. Connaughton, Ann Scott, M. Ellen Connaughton, T. Kelly, Ciss Brennan, K. Hartigan, Mrs Scott. 2nd row: Mona Brennan, Eileen Brennan, —, Anne O'Hara, Molly Finan, Mary Cahill. 1st row: Margaret Gaffney, Catherine Gaffney, Josie Egan, Agnes Conor —, —, —, —, Kate Durr, Chirs Brennan

*School Photo 1924 Margaret J Connaughton*
*(Third Row Back , 4th from left)*

*Mr & Mrs Dineen*

*Above:* Mr & Mrs Dineen's home at 16 Emmet Square, Clonakilty and Mrs Dineen (widow) with her six children and a neighbours child.

*Left:* Mrs Dineen with Baby Number One.

*Below:* Six Dineen Children growing up fast.

*Father John O'Hea (Clonakilty, Co Cork) arrived in Ibadan, Nigeria in 1961. John and his catechist, Andrew Ojo, are full of enthusiasm for the work of the Lord. His latest project is a new nursery/primary school in an area where education was never available. The Irish Government helped fund the project.*

*Past pupil Fr. John O'Hea SMA carries on the tradition founding a school where education was never available.*

*St. Mary's Munster Junior Football 'B' Champions 1962*

*Seated: (l. to r.): Pat Collins, Michael McCarthy, Bernard Harrington,
Flor Hayes (Capt.), Fachtna Murphy, Tom Sutton, Ted Hayes*

*Standing: (l. to r.): Tim F. Hayes, Joe O'Sullivan, Brian Calnan, Anthony
Cooke, Michael Mc Carthy, Noel O'Sullivan, Charlie Cullinane, Dan
Cullinane, Laurence Coughlan, Aidan O'Regan*

**Eloquent victory**

*St. Mary's College Debating Team
Winners of the 1977 EBS All-Ireland
Schools Debating Competition*

*Standing: (l. to r.): Jerome
O'Sullivan. Eddie Goggin
(Teacher/Coach),
Finbarr O'Donovan (Capt.)
Seated: (l. to r.) John Lyons,
Ray O'Donovan*

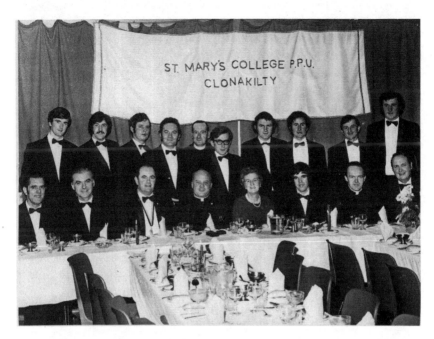

*1973 Reunion*

*St. Mary's College Past Pupil Union*

73

### Hall of Fame Award

*Mrs Dineen pictured receiving the Hall of Fame Trophy and above with
Sporting Legend, Moss Keane (R.I.P) and John L. O'Sullivan, T.D. (R.I P)*

*Bean Uí Dhuinnín pictured with past pupils (from left) Jerry Beechinor, Fr's. John Kingston & Jim Duggan & Michael O'Regan at the unveiling of a plaque in Astna St (Tom Sheehy's Hardware Store – the site of the original Coláiste Muire in 1938)*

## COLÁISTE MUIRE
## ST. MARY'S COLLEGE
### 1938 - 1980

THIS PLAQUE HAS BEEN COMMISSIONED BY THE PAST STUDENTS OF ST. MARY'S COLLEGE, CLONAKILTY TO PERPETUATE THE MEMORY OF:-

MR. JEREMIAH J. DINEEN B.Sc., H.Dip. in Ed. & MRS. MARGARET J. DINEEN B.A., B.Comm., H.Dip. in Ed.

WHO FOUNDED ST. MARY'S SECONDARY SCHOOL AT THIS PLACE IN 1938.

MOLADH AGUS BUÍOCHAS DÓIBH ARAON

*Corn Choláiste Muire*
*This is the trophy that past pupils presented to Mrs Dineen engraved with the name of the school '**chun ainm na scoile a choimeád beo**' and to be available for Glór na nGael competitions to promote the Irish language.*

*Selection of Class Reunions from Coláiste Muire*

*Graveside of the Late Margaret J. Dineen in Darrara, Clonakilty, Co. Cork*

# Part II

# 18 Pádraig Ó Callanáin (pupil 1940–1946)

*Pádraig Ó Callanáin writes recollections from the period 1940–1946 with the focus on Mrs Dineen.*

I finished national school in Darrara in 1940. Both my parents were dead at that stage and I was the youngest of five. Sometime during that year Fr. David Crowley, Catholic curate in Clonakilty came to our house, a few miles outside the town, to talk to my older brother and myself about a new secondary school which had been established in the town, two years previously. As a country boy I would rarely have visited the town and so I knew very little about it, least of all about a secondary school. Fr. Crowley must have been aware that I had some potential because he encouraged me to enrol, pointing out the advantages a secondary education would have for my future life. So it was agreed that I would go there. Subsequently, I sat for an entrance examination for a scholarship as I remember it took place in the Industrial Hall and as luck would have it I was the beneficiary. I clearly remember my first day at school; the junior classes were in the ladies' cloakroom and the seniors were in the gents' cloakroom across the dance hall. It was a strange experience, sitting at a desk for two people, and surrounded by strangers. Up at the front, behind a tall desk at a platform, sat the lady teacher, Miss Connaughton, and we were to address her as Miss. Two things struck me about her; she wore a black flowing gown and to my simple eyes, she was a smashing-looking girl. What a thought, at that early age for a rough country boy! That view was shared by a lot of the lads, I might add. As regards the gown, it remained with her as long as my term lasted. In fact I don't think we ever saw her in 'civies'. The funny thing was we did not know for ages that she had a Christian name until someone found out it was Jean, which we thought was cute and later that it was 'Margaret' which was the name she came to be generally known by though, of course, no student would ever dare mention her first name within earshot. To us the teacher was a person of whom we were in awe and in this totally new environment, we instinctively felt she was a person to be respected and obeyed. So all day and every day it was, 'Yes, Miss' or 'No, Miss'.

As I remember her, she was firm and fair. She had a strong, clear voice, with an accent so different from our West Cork way of talking. In our small, narrow world, we thought everybody spoke alike. We were a small class so she knew us all by name and she would not tolerate any nonsense or improper behaviour. Her eagle eye would spot any misdemeanour and where something warranted a stronger response, the offender was dispatched to Mr Dineen for suitable treatment. He was a man for whom good conduct and good behaviour were all important and his exercise of discipline, while decisive, was very fair and matched the offence. It must be said that the leather strap, sticking out of his back pocket, sent out a clear message, 'watch it or you are in big trouble'. We all quickly got that message

At the beginning, Miss Connaughton explained what secondary education was all about; that we were starting out on a new, long journey, with great opportunities ahead for those who worked hard. She encouraged us to make the big effort and not to waste valuable time. She told us about important exams and how we could make worthwhile careers in the years ahead. Through it all we could see she was a kind, caring person who wanted the best for us. So we got to grips with all the new subjects and got the hang of her teaching methods. During Playtime, we played football in the park and on fine days we used to notice, Miss C. and Mr D. sitting side by side on a step on the side of the Hall. We worked it out that maybe they were 'courting'. We weren't far off the mark because they got married some time in 1942.

When Miss C. got married, she moved to a different level as far as we were concerned. We felt she was now a different sort of person, calling for a new kind of respect and deference. It took us a good while to get accustomed to calling her Mrs instead of Miss. She noticed this and she smiled a lot at that. Over time we migrated to Bank Street and then to the house on the 'Hill', the old famine dispensary. I can't remember the dates but I found Bank Street house small and crowded. I associate it particularly with a 'new', hand-me-down black suit which I got around that time and I remember how thrilled I was when Mrs Dineen complimented me on my new 'rig-out'.

The climate on the hill was a bit on the Arctic side, due to its elevation and venerable age. The wind whistled and the draughts got to you from all angles. These were the war years and we were all accustomed to deprivations. We may have grumbled and groused but we came through unscathed. We were all in the same boat, teachers and pupils and there was no time for 'softies'.

I don't remember much about the arrival of the young Dineens or how long Mrs Dineen was missing but in our own simple and unsophisticated way we thought what an amazing person she was. She had to manage the babies and the house and still teach. Had she help? We never thought about that! Yet whatever the problems, difficulties and worries she may have had in the home scene (and I am sure there were many sleepless nights) none of these were apparent to us as she went about her teaching in a perfectly normal way. With a lifetime of experience behind me now I can only say, 'What a woman'!

I will always remember one incident which showed me what a really kind and caring person she was. In the park, near the Industrial Hall, I fell and cut my wrist on broken glass. With the blood pouring out, someone shouted for Mrs Dineen, (or was it Miss C?).She came running, rushed me into the school, washed, treated and bandaged the wound using soothing words and a motherly hug made me feel good and for days afterwards she would always ask me how my hand was doing. That gave me a clear understanding of her kind and gentle nature and I had a new respect for her.

I can certainly say I loved her classes. I never stopped to analyse why. Was it just herself or her teaching methods? I don't know. Somehow she had a way of making us think; to use our heads and intelligence in working out what made things tick and to understand what life was about, in a broad sense. She seemed to us to be a deeply religious person and when the church bell rang at noon, her class would stop as she led us in the recitation of the Angelus. I always remember how devoutly she genuflected at the words, 'the Word was made flesh'.

Her Christian Doctrine classes were full of meaning and to ensure we had a good grasp of the basics she would pose some serious and searching questions. That gave us a feeling that here was a person,-not just our teacher- who had a close, informed relationship with God and I have no doubt that influenced us in many ways. She introduced us also into an understanding of our Irish culture and language and encouraged us to use some Irish as a spoken language. For me personally she was an inspiration and aroused in me an abiding interest in our native language, which grew and blossomed over the years. Today, and I say this in no boastful way, I am equally at home in Irish as in English. Interestingly enough, when I met my wife she was a fluent Irish speaker so it was only natural that we brought up our children bilingually. Mrs Dineen sowed the seed and I reaped the harvest and I am forever grateful to her for that.

She never spared her time and efforts to further our education and likewise with Mr Dineen. Coming up to exams we had extra classes on Saturdays, church and bank holidays. Maybe we were not enamoured at the time, giving up our free days but it was a measure of their dedication and commitment that they sacrificed their own precious family time in our interests. When we got to Leaving Cert. Mrs Dineen did a lot to focus our interest and attention on the many opportunities open to us. I was fortunate to have several choices and later when pursuing third-level studies, she gave me glowing references and which were hugely beneficial.

Sometime during my time at St. Mary's, I had my first ever visit to the cinema. It probably had something to do with our English course, one of Shakespeare's plays possibly, and the matinee visit was organised by Mrs Dineen. I recall what a great thrill it was but apart from the occasion itself I have no other memory of that event.

## Arbour Day.

The year after the Leaving Cert, a number of boys who were awaiting getting jobs returned to the school. During that time something called an arbour day occurred. My recollections are vague but it was arranged that a small group of us would spend the day in a field near the school, on the Inchydoney road, digging holes and planting trees. Years afterwards, I recall passing that way and noticing a reasonable number of developing trees. I would dearly love to know the idea behind it all. I wonder is there anybody still around who might throw light on the subject?

Still in the post-Leaving Cert year, I think it was Mrs Dineen who encouraged us to learn some shorthand and typing skills. A typewriter appeared from somewhere and probably about six of us tried our hand at the keyboard. I don't think we were really interested and we spent more time chatting than typing. In some spell of horseplay the typewriter was knocked off the desk and the arm which moved the carriage was badly bent. Here is where our ingenuity came to the fore. Someone got a spanner from his bicycle tool kit and managed to remove the damaged arm from the machine. Somebody else sneaked out, got his bike and raced off to Danny Lordan's Forge where a perfect repair job was done. At some stage during all this, Mr Dineen looked in to see how we were getting on. He noticed nothing amiss. The machine was restored to full health and nobody in authority was ever the wiser.

Having left Clonakilty in 1947 to make my way in the world, I'm afraid I lost contact with the town, the school and all related events. Therefore it was a great surprise and a privilege to be invited, as one of the 'oldies', to the unveiling of the Plaque in Astna Square, in September

1993, to commemorate the foundation in 1938 of what was now known as St. Mary's College and to perpetuate the memory of those two heroic and visionary, educational pioneers, Margaret Connaughton and Jeremiah Dineen. At that historic moment, there came from nowhere a wonderful memory; I could hear the sound of the Baby Ford going up the hill to the school. It was uncanny! She gave a rousing speech and in reference to the plaque she said something like this, 'this makes it look as if I am dead but let me tell you I am very much alive'. What an indomitable spirit! At the 'do' later in Dunmore, I renewed acquaintance with Mrs Dineen after forty-six years. We had a great chat *'as Ghaeilge'* and I reminded her that my competence in the language was largely due to her influence all those years ago.

That occasion triggered a massive 'look back' for me, as a whole kaleidoscope of memories came flooding back like a tidal wave; thoughts and questions and reflections that had never surfaced before now almost overwhelmed me. Who were these two young teachers from far away who arrived in Clonakilty in 1938, a place unknown to them? Where did they come from? What was their motivation? I searched for answers to these questions which never bothered me during my school years. Digging deep, enlightenment came gradually. They were people of tremendous courage and foresight with a vision for the future of secondary education in an area which had none. Only the better-off people could afford to send their children to Boarding schools. They started from scratch with the minimum of resources and equipment. They had to spread the word. I wonder did they have the support or recognition of the Department of Education? Somehow they managed to expand and develop this wonderful project providing educational opportunities to boys from the general area who would otherwise have been deprived. Asking questions here and there told me a lot about these heroic people. We will probably never know the true extent of the blood, sweat, tears and sacrifices they endured to make life better for those of us who were privileged to be their students.

Sadly and tragically, Mr Dineen passed away in 1953. To my great regret, I did not know that until several years later. That left Mrs Dineen with a young family to rear and a school to run. Surely that is when the true character and spirit of the woman came to the fore. Lesser mortals might have collapsed under this burden. Undaunted by the enormous challenge, she faced up bravely to these responsibilities and successful school results are a fitting tribute to the fighting spirit of this great teacher and this great lady. If I may take liberties and misquote a one-time world statesman, 'never was so much done by one person for so many'. I'm pretty sure those words would echo the sentiments of generations of alumni of St. Mary's.

I'm sure Mrs Dineen shed many a tear when she called it a day and retired from active service after forty-two years of devoted teaching. If I was around then I would have said, '*Míle, Míle buíochas duit, Bean Uí Dhuinnín, go mbeidh blianta sona sásta agat tar éis obair dícheallach na scoilíochta. Tá an saol seo fágtha aici anois.*' Now she enjoys the glories and wonders of Paradise, re-united with her beloved husband. I'm sure she swaps stories and experiences with some former past pupils who, like her, have gone to their eternal reward. *Suaimhneas síorraí ortha go léir.*

## 19 Michael Minihan RIP (pupil 1940s)

We had our first class in Astna Square; then we moved to Bank Street; then to the Industrial Hall, and after that to '*an Cnoc*'. When I first saw Mrs Dineen, I thought she was the most beautiful girl I had ever seen. I fell in love with her. All the class were in love with her. She is still very beautiful.

People talk about no jobs being available today but at that time there was nothing at all, neither guards nor civil service nor banks nor anything; but thanks to Mrs Dineen she made a fair job of some of us.

When I left her school I was in for a job with 250 others hoping for the same job and I got it.

## 20 Noreen Minihan (widow of Michael)

My beloved husband, Michael R.I.P., always spoke of Mrs Dineen with admiration, respect, appreciation and gratitude. When he finished primary school, there was no secondary education for boys in Clonakilty. The technical school was the only second-level school, catering for boys. Michael was awarded a half scholarship to a Boarding school in Roscrea but times were tough then and he was unable to avail of it.

"Miss Connaughton's" arrival in Clonakilty opened a whole new world to him and like-minded boys. "She was the most beautiful girl I ever saw," he would recall. "We all fell in love with her!" Michael was one of the first small group of students that attended the inaugural classes. The boys of Clonakilty owe a huge debt of gratitude to those pioneers of education. They had the vision to offer secondary education to the boys of the area, without having to leave home. Mr and Mrs Dineen and indeed the teachers they employed, were totally dedicated to their work as they imparted knowledge and a love of learning to their pupils. Their students could now face the future with confidence. They could compete for positions where secondary education was essential and they had a foundation whereby they were better fitted to take their place in society. Yes, the men of Clonakilty remember 'Mrs Dineen' with deep affection and much gratitude.

For myself, personally, I have fond memories of conversations with Mrs Dineen, as we would stop for a chat on the street. She spoke with clear precise diction, had an acute sense of humour, with a special smile and laugh. I clearly remember the night she was interviewed on television. The Urban Council in Clonakilty wanted to refurbish Emmet Square, where Mrs Dineen lived and present it as an example of a true

Georgian Square. The gardens were laid out, the houses got a face-lift and the doors, with their beautiful fan-lights were painted. The interviewer asked Mrs Dineen what she thought about it. "Very nice", she said, "my door is painted toastel green. I don't like it but it's what Billy Houlihan wanted!" To the very end she would comply with what was good for Clonakilty.

On Michael's behalf, "Thank you, Mrs Dineen!" *Ar dheis lámh Dé, go raibh tú.*

## 21 Jerry Lyons (pupil 1940s)

Sincere good wishes and congratulations! You and Mr Dineen opened up a whole new world for us when we took those first tentative steps to the big house on the hill. My best friendships have started and continued from St. Mary's; in the school and later on through the Past Pupils Union. I still quote some of the wise anecdotes of the late Mr Dineen.

## 22 Fr. Michael Scully (pupil 1946–1947)

My time at St. Mary's school was really very short, less than eighteen months and even during that time my attendance at school was less than laudable. However, my abiding memory of Mrs Dineen is that she was a very dedicated teacher, a very competent teacher, a teacher of integrity who through her classes and commitment to her pupils/students had the capacity to inspire students to strive not only for academic success but also for the attainment of social and moral values to underpin a worthwhile lifestyle.

I left St. Mary's in March 1947 and I did not meet Mrs Dineen again until sometime towards the end of the century, so possibly fifty or more years had elapsed! I called to see her one day at her home in The Square, Clonakilty. She received me very graciously and I might say happy that I had called. It was a special kind of visit for me and now a memory that I treasure!

Trusting everything goes well for all of you involved in the project.

## 23 Dan Linnane (pupil 1944–1950)

I'm delighted to be here tonight to honour St. Mary's and Mrs Dineen, on behalf of the lads of 1944–1950 period, the time of the second World War and its aftermath. It was a time of scarcity and poverty was very common and rationing strictly enforced. For most people, their education finished after national school as most parents could not afford to send their children to boarding school. There was a good convent secondary school for girls, but none for boys in the town. So many, many people were delighted when Mr and Mrs Dineen decided to set up St. Mary's. The early days were not easy for them as there were many calls on limited resources but the words 'can't' or 'quit' never appeared in their lexicon. They were a great team and soon the college grew from strength to strength, aided by good results and dare I say it, 'good pupils and of whom they were proud and in whom they imbued the highest moral standards.

My days in St. Mary's were by and large very happy though at times we saw some falling standards and indiscretions. We had some wonderful teachers but I am sure most of you will agree that Mrs Dineen was the best. I often wondered was it because she was the only woman on the staff and as Michael said she was so beautiful. She was kind, witty, understanding and was a wonderful communicator. She gave praise where it was due but could give the idler a right good tongue-lashing that could set him cringing. However, if you went too far a visit to Mr Dineen might be necessary with sometimes painful results. However, he too was essentially a very gentle man.

Our leisure activities, in those days were taken up with hurling, football and handball.

I'm very happy to be associated with this tribute to St. Mary's and Mrs Dineen, without whom our quality of life would have been very different.

## 24 Seán Ó Coileáin (pupil 1950s)

"Mrs Dineen" – What a woman! What an outstanding person she was, what memories, emotions, gratitude and emulation that name conjures up for generations of grateful West Cork men throughout the length and breadth of Ireland and beyond.

What a show she ran! What other person could have managed, educated, controlled and guided a school full of teenage young 'bucks' so successfully, for so many years. This she did, entirely single-handedly since the unfortunate, premature passing of her husband, Jerry in 1953.

I attended St. Mary's during the fifties. I was part of the 1950- 1955 crop. This period was a particularly traumatic one for the Dineen family. By the early fifties, Jerry and Margaret Dineen, having travelled a long and arduous road together, since they had founded St. Mary's, seemed now finally to have attained a new plateau in their lives. They could boast a most successful school, a fine house in Emmet Square and most importantly six beautiful children. Being people of strong faith they were deeply grateful to the Lord for all these blessings.

However, I think it was when tragedy struck in 1953 that Mrs Dineen showed her true character and mettle. Just as the future seemed to promise happiness and security, Jerry Dineen was diagnosed with cancer. I have particular memories of the period that Mr Dineen was hospitalised. Despite this most shattering blow, Mrs Dineen stuck resolutely with her task. In spite of everything she scarcely missed a day at St. Mary's. During all that time 'her boys' got regular updates on the progress of Mr Dineen's illness, in particular how 'Mr Dineen's daily reception of Holy Communion and his deep faith helped them both to be resigned to whatever the future held in store'. There were days when she struggled to keep her composure on the rostrum. There were times when she struggled to keep from nodding. But she soldiered on and kept up a brave front.

During those final weeks there was actually more of a family atmosphere in St. Mary's. When finally Mr Dineen succumbed to his illness, his loss was palpable and personal to us all. However while missing that noble and upright man who was Jerry Dineen, even more so, we felt a deep empathy with Mrs Dineen in her awful loss and the daunting task that now lay ahead of her. From a joint and loving venture and the prospect of raising their family and managing the now established and very successful St. Mary's College together in the years ahead, she was now alone. What a year previously promised to be a joint and joyful prospect now became a lonely and daunting challenge. But, my God how Mrs Dineen rose to that challenge; as I said at the outset, 'What a woman! And to take liberty with the words of John D. Sheridan 'the rest is history'.

What impressionable teenager could not have been influenced for life by the absolute integrity of character, depth of faith, sincerity, steadfastness and diligence of that woman?

*"Mrs Dineen, you will always be fondly remembered and most highly and gratefully regarded by your loving family and by all of us 'your boys' of St. Mary's on the Hill.*

*Is cinnte go bhfuil tú féin agus Diarmuid le chéile anois in áit speisialta i measc na naomh sna flaithis. Gura fada buan do chuimhne"*

# 25 Tom Cooney R.I.P (teacher 1955–1961)

It was my first job. I enjoyed my years in Clonakilty very much and I learned how to do my job. St. Mary's College will always be a big part of my history.

# 26 Mrs Una Flynn R.I.P (teacher 1960s)

I came in the early sixties and I was the first science teacher. It was a challenging task and I am very grateful to Mrs Dineen for all her help and encouragement during those early years. Mrs Dineen was a very dedicated teacher. I have very happy memories of St. Mary's.

# 27 Gerald Walsh (pupil 1948–1953, teacher 1957–1961)

I had been a student from 1948–1953 and I taught there from 1957–1961. It was my first job and I learned a great deal for the later years of my teaching career. This school had done a lot for the people of West Cork. I'm very glad to be here tonight and I'm delighted to have the opportunity to pay tribute to the founders of St. Mary's College.

# 28 Michael O'Keeffe (teacher 1954–1956)

It was my first job, 1954, 1955 and 1956. (She's advising me now to keep out from the microphone, she was always advising me.) It was my first job in 1954. She gave me great assistance and it was something I always appreciated. We hear a lot today about teachers being stressed but when I heard Mrs Dineen earlier today, she was going, going, going, just as she used to in 1954. I don't know how she did it but she did. I would like to wish you, Mrs Dineen, many blessings.

## 29 Charlie Cullinane (pupil)

Mrs Dineen, I would like to add my tribute and respects to your life, devotion and career, given to the people of Clonakilty and for all you have done for Clonakilty and for all of us past students, in particular. Congrats and good luck for another fifty years.

## 30 Michael Pattwell (pupil 1958–1963)

At that time the school fees were £12, (later raised to £15). It wasn't a lot of money but in those days and for some families it was hard enough to get it together but Mrs Dineen never said it <u>had</u> to be in before such or such a time. She waited until it came. She sort of trusted you to bring it sooner or later. We, (our family) did appreciate her attitude in this.

French and physics were introduced to the school at this stage. I remember Mrs Dineen, who taught us commerce, speaking on the concept of a European market. There was no EEC (European Economic Community) at this time but Mrs Dineen had the foresight to know that this would come about in the future and I remember her explaining this to us.

## 31 Fr. Jerome McCarthy BSc, PhD.

Mrs Dineen stands out as the single most remarkable woman I've ever encountered, and in the fifty years since my Leaving Cert, I've met many impressive women. She had a passion to give *real* education to us boys and the record shows her success. Because I must be brief, I'll just mention one memory; she took us after school hours to her home to listen to Shakespeare. As a result, I developed a love for Shakespeare and can rattle off reams of him to this day. If it was now, I can imagine her using DVDs instead of LPs and a website to make sure we did our homework. She was tough on us but we loved her, still do.

## 32 Fr. John Kingston, CSSp (pupil 1960s)

Greetings from Rome. I am delighted that somebody has got going to pay tribute to Mrs Margaret Dineen, that great woman. The book will not only be a tribute looking back at who she was and did but also a way to quarry some of the wealth of human greatness that she brought into the lives of so many people in Clonakilty, many of us now wandering far from there. I am sure that not even her son, Sean, with all his mathematical genius could calculate how much she has influenced the lives of generations of people through her work in education.

She was the quintessential great woman who multitasked, long before the expression was invented. Even as boys then, we had to marvel at her grit and her skills. She was a faithful mother whose children were at school with us. As boys, we knew that such a real mother could not be fooled by our antics. She had a wonderful natural authority and when young, inexperienced male teachers could barely control their class, all she had to do was appear at the back of the room and things became very businesslike.

Among her many aspects which impressed me was her 'no nonsense' way of living her faith. If she had the first class in the morning she would recite the rosary with no frills, fairly fast but with profound respect. Even with those ten minutes gone, she still seemed to have ample time to teach us some wonderful '*seanfhocail*', of which I wish I remembered more now. She was a natural teacher and that, for her pupils was surely a great asset. How she managed the school and the teaching staff I do not know but it seemed seamless to me which of course it must not have been. Ireland in the fifties and sixties may have been a land flowing with milk and honey but certainly not with milk and money. She managed and also raised a wonderful family.

Ever since I left that school and found myself in many great institutes of learning like UCD, Trinity College, London University, I have always been proud to tell people that I attended a small day secondary school co-founded by the woman who ran it on her own, at the time I was a student there.

When the French Holy Ghost Fathers applied to come to work in Dublin in 1859, Cardinal Cullen, who was the then Archbishop told them they could come but they must do something about secondary education for boys which he said was in a low state in the country. They accepted and a year later founded Blackrock College and other schools later. When Margaret J. Dineen and her husband started their little secondary school in Clonakilty, it would be an understatement to say that boys' secondary education in the town and area was in difficulties. There was none. As I have discovered in my time in very poor parts of the world as a missionary, poverty is the greatest scourge and education is the most powerful instrument in overcoming it. There is no doubt that the visionary work of Margaret Dineen and her husband was a decisive factor in the progress of people in Clonakilty and the surrounding countryside.

I greatly look forward to reading the proposed book on one of Clonakilty's great heroes and I thank you for undertaking to produce it.

## 33 Traolach Ó Donnabháin (pupil 1960s)

Looking back now with the hindsight of the experience of many other teachers and lecturers from the primary, secondary and third-level sectors, I am of the opinion that Mrs Dineen was one of that rare breed of educators who loved her profession and whose dedication to and hard work on its behalf knew no bounds. She had a practical, hands-on approach to teaching and she used her wide knowledge of the subject matter and her vast experience, constantly built up during her career, to impart the course content in a practical way by the use of numerous examples and by engaging the students personally, regardless of their ability, rather than just following the textbook on the subject.

She saw any disruptive behaviour in class as infringing on that endeavour and she reacted to it immediately. If it continued, her agitation grew. I well remember Mrs Dineen's 'tongue lashings', saliva flying as her agitation grew, until finally, if all else failed, the breakdown in tears. That invariably worked with even the toughest characters. Prior to 1963, when Éamonn McGrath joined the staff and subsequently became 'Dean of Discipline' she had to administer the discipline herself. Her generosity and humanity are well demonstrated by the fact that, as in my own family's case when three of us were attending St. Mary's together in the mid-1960s, my mother was given a substantial reduction in the school fees. I know that also applied to other families and I am also aware that some fees were not paid and the matter was not pursued.

She also awarded a scholarship annually to the individual achieving the highest marks in the entrance exam and the subsequent first and second Year Department of Education exams to help alleviate the costs. I was fortunate to win the scholarship for two years. She gave many 'free gratis grinds' after school hours, both at St. Mary's and at 16 Emmet Square as required, to ensure that as many students as possible passed the Leaving Cert exams. In my own case, when school progress 'slipped' on occasion, my mother got some 'notes' from Mrs Dineen on the matter! I am sure many other mothers were similarly addressed.

The old 'Fever Hospital' on the Youghals road was cold and draughty and literally shook in a gale of wind. Class room facilities were minimal. There was no science block up to the late sixties. While the average intake to first year in the mid-sixties was of the order of 20-25, yet only fourteen registered for my first year in 1961, the smallest class of the time. Some of us walked from 'town', while others cycled from places as far away as Rosscarbery, Rossmore, Timoleague and Barryroe, yet rarely missed a day even during the winter. Due to our small numbers, we occupied the small classroom on the first floor, opposite the 'teachers meeting room' (the corridor), for the full five years. We were right over the flat of Jackie and Mary Kate Cunningham (Lowney), the downstairs tenants and the smell of cooking and the sound of piano playing, constantly wafted up to our nostrils and eardrums.

The massive difference between primary and secondary school became clear to us early on. While we had a good grounding in the 'three R's' together with an introduction to history and geography, the range and depth of the subjects, the formal timetable, change of teacher for each subject, range of textbooks and the sheer volume of work was all new to us. We were also in the company of 'men' aged 18-19 who were doing Leaving Cert. The 'leather' replaced the stick for punishment. I would estimate that there were up to ninety students in the college in 1961, spread between the five years. During the Inter. Cert year, we stayed on for a study period from 4 p.m. to 6 p.m. Those in need of grinds got them, free of charge, of course, either at school or at Mrs Dineen's House. During my years at St. Mary's, the vast majority of the students passed the Inter and Leaving exams with a good percentage achieving honours level. In addition to *an Ghaeilge,* she taught history and commerce to Inter Cert and continued Irish and commerce to Leaving Cert students.

I recall in 1965, the Department of Education introduced a new Leaving Cert maths syllabus. This put an extraordinary unfair burden on pupils and teachers alike as the 1966 Leaving Class had only one year in which to study the new syllabus. Mrs Dineen insisted we would sit the 'old' syllabus exam paper in 1965 and the 'new' in 1966. Many of us passed both, but we were denied the opportunity of achieving honours maths in 1966.

For the 1962 Munster Colleges Junior 'B' football championships, Barry Patterson and Tom Flynn entered a team from the school for the first time. Flor Hayes, who had won an all-Ireland medal with Cork in 1961, captained the team. He narrowly missed a senior medal with Cork against Meath in 1967, following a marvellous personal game. Flor was one of the most skilful footballers to ever grace Croke Park. His brother, Tim F., himself a great player, played for the Cork minors in the mid-sixties for three consecutive years and only narrowly missed a medal. There were fifteen heroes on that team who won the championship that year. We all contributed to the cost of the 'black and white' jerseys and had some great bus trips to the various matches. The College played in the championship for a number of years afterwards, but the 1962 victory was never repeated. I was a 'sub' on those post'62 teams and played as a half-forward. It is an interesting historical fact that the Clon Senior football team that contested the 1968 County Final against Carbery contained some fourteen players who had been pupils of St. Mary's.

In 1977, our entire family travelled to the Abbey Theatre in Dublin, to witness St. Mary's debating team, coached by Eddie Goggin and Éamonn McGrath and captained by my brother Finbarr, win the EBS all-Ireland schools' debating competition.

Mrs Dineen had been teaching classes of young men since 1938. I doubt that there was a trick or antic she hadn't encountered in her career! While naturally concerned for our welfare and having to take a strong line in dealing with each incident, I'm pretty sure that overall she accepted that most were of the 'mischievous, high spirits' variety. Following each 'tongue-lashing', I'm sure the incidents were quickly forgotten. I don't remember her bearing a long term grudge against any student.

Every year had its share of 'characters' and ours was no exception. Looking back now, some of the stunts we pulled are hardly credible. One day, after lunch, we rounded up some half dozen of Georgie Nugent's (the adjacent neighbour) young bonhams and released them on the top floor. They mainly rolled down the flight of stairs, squealing and messing past a speechless Mrs Dineen on the first floor. On another occasion, we led Georgie Nugent's brown 'cob' into the stairwell on the ground floor and watched for the reaction of the teachers as they arrived, after lunch, to see a horse's rear end facing them. We 'jacked up' teacher's cars and blocked the way down the hill with pieces of machinery from Nugent's yard. The excuses given for being late were sometimes novel. During the study period for the Inter Cert, we used every trick to 'disappear', especially during the fine weather. We regularly cycled to Inchydoney for a game of football. On one occasion, we learned of the local convent secondary school's sports day. We had exhausted every excuse by this time to get away. As luck would have it, Padraig Walsh, (a contractor on the Western Road where Pat Sullivan now operates) was repairing the roof and had scaffolding erected past our window up to the roof. So when the teacher was absent for a few minutes, there was a mass exodus through the window and down the ladders and platforms of the scaffolding to the ground! We made our presence felt at the sports that day. The nuns complained bitterly to Mrs Dineen and following a good tongue-lashing where we were all called 'tinkers', we were rigidly monitored after that.

In 1980 when the school closed and was amalgamated into the new Community College, the Committee of the Festival of West Cork honoured Mrs Dineen with the West Cork Hall of Fame award for a lifetime of dedication to secondary education in Clonakilty.

Apart from her dedication to teaching generally, her love of and the emphasis she placed on *an Ghaeilge,* had a major influence on me subsequently. Since returning to Clonakilty in the mid-1980s, I have been involved in local branches of *Glór na nGael* and *Conradh na Gaeilge* and in founding a now very successful *Gaelscoil* and *Meánscoil* to Junior Cert level. Mrs Dineen was always involved in the various national competition adjudications and awarding of the various prizes. In 1988, I approached her (then in her late seventies) to conduct an evening class, *as Ghaeilge*, for adults. So, for two years, during the early 1990's, she conducted a *Rang Ghaeilge* for adults, every Tuesday night at the Boy's Infant school and never missed a Tuesday night, no matter what the weather conditions. One particularly wet night as I drove her home, I politely enquired if she wished to continue during the winter. Her immediate response was, "I would go back teaching full-time in the morning, given the opportunity".

Many past pupils contributed to an active PPU (Past Pupils' Union) over the years and I attended a number of functions on returning to Clonakilty, particularly the 50th anniversary of the founding of the college in 1988 and the sixtieth in 1998. Mrs Dineen herself attended both functions. All her past pupils, whether in the universities, the professions, the world of business, the religious life or a myriad of other careers, at home or abroad, are today united by a bond that stretches back to St. Mary's. Their contributions to their various careers and the societies in which they live are the legacy of St. Mary's and in a special way of Mrs Dineen. In 1993, the PPU presented *Glór na nGael* with the *Corn Choláiste Muire*. Mrs Dineen proudly presented the trophy to the annual winners of the *Comórtas Lucht Ghnó Áitiúil* for a number of years afterwards. In June, 1996, when Professor Lee officially opened the *Gaelscoil,* founded by *Glór na nGael,* Mrs Dineen was one of the distinguished guests. I recall her profound pride and joy on that occasion.

My generation will always be indebted to Mrs Dineen for our secondary education.

*Bhí sé de phribhléid is d'onóir domsa, im dhuine fásta, bheith páirteach i thuilleadh forbairt na Gaeilge, le Bean Uí Dhuinnín, i gCloch na gCoillte 'sna 1990's.*

# 34 Mícheál Ó Ríogáin (pupil 1960s)

From the beginning I was taken under her wing, like an adopted son. Every pupil was treated as an individual and this approach certainly paid dividends for me, in later years. She was well organised, decisive when the occasion demanded, possessed a sharp intellect, exercising the skill and ability to command one's attention at all times and adopting a positive approach to the subject matter or related issues. She would frequently quote relevant examples of national or local interest to illustrate a point, which could be quite graphic, colourful and sometimes humorous. I was very much influenced by her strong faith. This was demonstrated by her daily devotion to Saint Joseph of Cupertino and also by the occasional retreats conducted in the school by Religious Orders. She encouraged fasting during Lent and on one occasion quoted an example from Bishop Lucey's Lenten Pastoral which advocated refraining from opening the morning mail until lunch time, as an act of self-denial.

Her Irish classes were equally life-giving and this fact was greatly enhanced by her outstanding voice projection, always loud and clear, with every syllable distinctly audible as if she was giving a lesson in elocution. Personally, I soon discovered that I was now loving a language that I had previously dreaded. For me it was the icing on the cake, thanks to Margaret J. Dineen- the teacher. She was the jewel in the crown, a genius in our midst and magic in our eyes. *"An rud is anamh, is iontach."* What is strange is wonderful. But why so strange to meet a woman, fully alive, using all the gifts and talents God gave her, to the utmost of her ability!

# 35 John Healy (pupil 1966)

Delighted to see Mrs Dineen being honoured in this way. I was influenced by her in that I saw her drive and ambition in running the college and her sincere wish and hope that all her students would get on in life and fulfil their potential.

A short story from 1966, Saturday morning double maths class, first period with Mr McDonnell, (remember him driving the small white Fiat 600 each day from Monkstown, Cork). This particular Saturday morning, we were to study theorem 29, 'pietagerous' the square on the 'highpotenuse'. I hated Geometry, could never understand it and what it was needed for. Of course, McDonnell called on me to recite the theorem and needless to say I failed miserably. He pulled out the leather strap and gave me six of the best on each hand, with the threat of being called on again at the maths class on Monday. He also mentioned that he was in a hurry to go home as soon as school was over as he had a wedding in Cork. The clock said 12.30 and I had organised two look-outs to keep an eye for him coming in the car. Meanwhile, in the short time available, I pulled down from the ditch every stone I could find to block the road and delay his departure to the wedding. We went down to watch the fun from behind the local GAA pitch wall and saw him heaving all the stones to the side. We had a good laugh at his expense.

On Monday morning I was called out of class and asked to report to Mrs Dineen's office. Mr McDonnell was there also and I was asked to explain my actions on the previous Saturday. My first reaction was that someone had 'ratted' on me and I swore vengeance on the traitor until I discovered that 'the Missus' had seen all from the top window of the school and I was caught red-handed. Mr McDonnell went to town on me for the rest of the year and I paid dearly for my stonework.

I wish you all well with the publication and I look forward to reading the book.

# 36 Con Hodnett (pupil 1960s)

It was great to reminisce on forty-six years ago and my youthful days in St. Mary's. Mrs Dineen was inspiring, smart, fair, friendly and always helpful. I count my blessings to have known her for an enlightening education and for life skills. She taught me how to be a respectful and loyal citizen and always to be honourable, honest and truthful. Now, thanks to her, like a good movie, my life is cast with wonderful, lovable characters whom I have met along the way.

# 37 Charles McCarthy (pupil 1960s)

I remember, as a first year student, having to pass through Leaving Cert. class to get to our classroom and if one was late, as happened sometimes, one caught a glimpse of Mrs Dineen, teaching the Leaving Certs, big men like Michael Patwell and Tim F. Hayes, who were twice her size and they were like putty in her hands. I often wondered what was the cause of the awe Mrs Dineen had over these big giants!

# 38 Fachtna McCarthy (pupil 1968–1973)

So far everybody has been so complimentary that one would almost believe that this woman here was a saint. I will tell you a story now which shows another aspect. My brother had just left school and he was telling Mrs Dineen that I would be coming soon so he said, half in earnest, 'I hope he will do better than I did?' and Mrs Dineen's reply was immediate: 'Yes, I should hope so too.'

She really was one of the most wonderful people I have ever known and she gave us a wonderful education. I would like to thank Mrs Dineen sincerely for all she did.

In responding to the request to contribute to the book on the life of the late Mrs Margaret Dineen I am mindful of the fact that there will be large numbers who will focus on her achievements, her teaching skills and her love of Irish, among many other things. In those circumstances I have decided to contribute an article which focuses on St. Mary's College Past Pupil's Union, an organisation that was dear to her heart.

I had the honour of serving as chairman of the PPU for approximately eight years. During all of that time the main function of the organisation was to arrange the annual dinner dance, usually held on Saint Stephen's Day or New Year's Eve. It was generally accepted as being one of the social highlights of the year in Clonakilty. Mrs Dineen always attended and clearly took pride in seeing so many of her past pupils making the effort to be present. She made it clear that she felt honoured that so may people took such obvious pride in their former school. As each year passed the list of achievements of her past pupils seemed to grow longer and more and more former pupils were seen to have distinguished themselves in a great variety of fields. Despite the relatively modest surroundings in which they had been educated, the past pupils of St. Mary's School had gone on to hold down many important positions. Mrs Dineen felt immensely proud of the role she had played, but was too modest to claim any of the credit. She would invariably comment that the student under discussion had "worked hard", or had "shown great dedication". The praise would be for the student. She never sought to claim any of the credit for herself, though, in many cases, it was richly deserved. On the occasion of the annual dinner dance she would have the opportunity to show the witty and light hearted side to her character, something that was not always obvious to the students while they were attending the school. Her wit was sharp on occasions, but always well intentioned. She displayed a keen interest in the PPU and was deeply appreciative of the efforts of those who served on its committee. The task of keeping it alive became more difficult in the

1980s, after the school closed, and was replaced by the new Community College. There was no influx of new members. Many of the older members found it more difficult to remain involved. This was because the PPU was more than about the organising of an annual dinner dance. During the 1970s the PPU had, in conjunction with four other organisations, become involved in running the weekly dances in the Industrial Hall. This had proved to be a wise decision. The venture was extremely successful, leading to the situation where, for a decade or more, that hall was one of the most successful dance venues in the country. Considerable sums of money were raised and the PPU was in a position, on an annual basis, to make contributions to various deserving charities. The PPU was widely praised for its generosity and role in the community. Running the dances made serious demands on the members each week. As time went by this commitment became harder to sustain. In addition, changing social habits saw the slow demise of the traditional dance hall. In the mid-1980s, with funding becoming more and more difficult, and no new members coming on stream, the decision was taken by the small committee still remaining to wind up the affairs of the PPU. The decision was reluctantly taken. By now, a whole new generation of young boys had been educated in the new Community College and the old St. Mary's School building had become little more than a curiosity for many.

As I look back, a quarter of a century after the winding up of the PPU, and almost forty years after leaving the school, I am immensely proud to have been a past pupil and to have played a role in the PPU. I made many friends during my student days in the school and my involvement in the PPU. I recall the late Mrs Dineen with fondness and affection. It was a privilege to have known her and to have been educated by her. She was a unique character, shaped by her love of education and devotion to educating others. I still recall her love of Irish in particular. With each passing year I have an even deeper appreciation of her achievements, particularly in the light of her personal circumstances. Having been widowed at a young age, and with a family to rear, she still found time to play the fullest possible role as the driving force behind the school that was to play such an important role in the lives of so many in Clonakilty, for close on half a century.

## 39 Eddie Goggin (teacher 1970s)

'A woman of substance' is how best to describe the late Mrs Margaret Dineen. She was a tough, hardworking and energetic lady and an extremely good role model for her students where work ethic was concerned. She had a job to do as Principal, teacher, wife and mother and she excelled in all. She demanded the same level of commitment and dedication from her staff and pupils as she gave herself. That's why St. Mary's was such an outstanding school because most sang from the same 'Mrs Dineen hymn sheet'.

Conditions in the school were fairly spartan and on a more negative note it was a pity she didn't show a little more understanding and compassion where working conditions like heating and the like were concerned. We often left the building, in the middle of winter close to being blue in colour. Overall, I have fond memories of the lady. May she rest in peace.

## 40 John Lyons (pupil 1970s)

I refer to your correspondence regarding proposed book to be published on the life of Mrs Dineen. Firstly, it is only right and fitting that a book is be published on Mrs Dineen; her contribution to education in Clonakilty and the wider catchment area is immense and has indeed left a mark on us all who were lucky enough to attend her school.

Due to pressure of work and the fact that I am currently at an advanced stage of a personal project i.e. PhD in Sociology, I am unable to contribute a written submission at this time. Tennyson stated that 'knowledge comes but wisdom lingers'. Mrs Dineen's wisdom has touched all those who were privileged and indeed lucky enough to have attended St. Mary's College. Her courage, ethics and determination to complete her project, in difficult circumstances highlighted her strength of character. She was the 'Peig Sayers' of our time, whose survival instincts ensured the continuation of education and excellent edification within her community. The sense of community and of being part of something special was very evident among the students of St. Mary's.

The very best to everyone involved in this project.

## 41 Donal O'Leary (pupil 1970s)

All the boys were potential leaders. They were all equal. I sat for the entrance exam with Mrs Dineen presiding from her large desk. It was intimidating, being in the shadow of my older brother, who possessed a natural ability for brilliance and was admitted the previous year. My mother's love was realised through tenacity and determination. Many sacrifices were made. I had to succeed.

I first encountered Mrs Dineen while we were collecting milk and she was collecting eggs at our neighbouring farm. I did not realise then the impact that "the Mrs" would have on me in years to come. As a mentor, Mrs Dineen was determined that her students would reach for the higher goal.

Mrs Dineen would march from class to class, handbag under her arm, teaching Irish history, Irish literature and then on to accounting with an unwavering commitment. She founded St. Mary's College with her husband and tirelessly carried on their dream after his death. Her dedication to her students and the high standard she expected in return never ceased. It is still inspiring.

## 42 Finbarr O'Donovan (1976-1980)

A most marvellous woman. We can all thank her for the education, for the camaraderie, for the friendships we made there and for the achievements some of us subsequently made.

Early in the morning, we would be working out what free class we would have in the day. If it was the 3–4 p.m. period, we might manage to get home at 3 o'clock but Mrs Dineen would make sure that this would never happen. We worked out a scheme whereby two of the lads, acting as scouts, would tiptoe very quietly out of the room, to check that the coast was clear, then down the stairs while the rest of us followed like mice; then just at the last two steps, the two scouts would make a big noise, out comes Mrs Dineen, the scouts got off but the rest of us had to go back up to class until 4 o'clock.

I thank you so much, Mrs Dineen, for all you have done for all of us. I wish you very many happy years.

## 43 Fr. John Paul Hegarty (1970s)

For me to try to assess the value and the influence of your life on the many thousands of pupils who passed through the doors of your school over the years would be well-nigh impossible. It was a reason for deep gratitude from all of us as, in one way or another, each of us experienced the love that God has for each and every one of us. Through your life and your teaching career, during the years that you spent in the school here in

Clonakilty, you treated each one of us with the utmost respect and dignity. You had a deep interest in each pupil who passed through the doors of your school. You knew each one of us by name and that meant an awful lot to us. On a personal note, I can truly say that you taught me truth, hope, justice and love. You taught me to believe in God and to believe in myself. I pay tribute to you and I thank you that you touched my life and that you were such a profound influence on my life and on the lives of all who had the privilege of attending St. Mary's.

# 44 Martin Condon (pupil 1975-1980)

**The last day**

It was mid-June and as always the weather was 'splitting the stones' as the final countdown to my final Leaving Cert exam, physics, approached. I remember the global news being dominated by the controversy over the Olympic Games in Moscow and whether the U.S. would boycott the games or not. Also, the U.S. primary elections were underway with the main focus on the challenge of Senator Edward Kennedy to the incumbent President Jimmy Carter to win the Democratic nomination.

We were all aware though that St. Mary's would close for the final time at the end of the exams and a new era of education would begin in Clonakilty the following September with the opening of the Community College, drawing students from St. Mary's and from the Vocational School.

However, our focus that hot June of 1980 was entirely on the Leaving Certificate exams and day by day things moved on until that final morning arrived when a small handful of us walked up the hill and sat down for that final physics paper. To be honest, I remember very little about the exam itself; physics was never my strong point and I was just glad to get it over with.

As we left the room, as always, Mrs Dineen awaited us and, as ever, was deeply interested in how we had done and if we ' had liked the paper'. At that stage, I don't think many of us were in for a thorough post-mortem but I remember being very conscious that, now the exams were concluded, the doors of St. Mary's would be shut for the final time and a colourful era of secondary education would draw to a close in Clonakilty.

Nowadays, I guess, the closure of a secondary school would be big news in a country town with media presence, photographers and local politicians etc. about the place to mark such an auspicious occasion. But 1980 was a different time in a different Ireland and it was all so low key and utterly reflective of Mrs Dineen's approach; yet, in hindsight, it must have been quite an emotional time for her as well. However, Mrs Dineen was in fine form that day and I remember asking her if she would mind if I could take a souvenir of the school with me and she had no difficulty with that and that is why the duster from our long-standing classroom, at the top of the building, ended up in the farmhouse in Ballinascarty that evening!

So, exams finally finished and farewells said, we happily set off down that hill for the last time and, duster in hand, we prepared to head out into the big wide world, full of the confidence of youth and of our hopes for the future. In the distance, we could see the scaffolding on the new building that, in a few months would herald the commencement of a new era of secondary education in Clonakilty.

# Appendix 1
# Eamonn McGrath R.I.P. (teacher 1963–1980)

*Extract from St. Mary's P.P.U. commemorative booklet 1980.*

## Part I

Some years ago, half a dozen of us were sitting around a conference table in the Dept. of Education, endeavouring to arrive at a consensus on the marking of the Leaving Cert. Honours English paper. During a lull, while the chief advising examiner was engaged on the phone, a colleague leaned over and asked me: "Do the teachers at St. Mary's still stand at the window on the first floor corridor, during the morning break, and grumble about the cold and lack of facilities?" Before I could recover sufficiently to answer, he smiled and said, 'I taught there in the fifties, you know. It was quite an experience!' He went on to elaborate on the many rigours of that experience- with most of which I was already familiar.

When he had finished I was able to assure him that, while teachers still grumbled about the cold – amongst other and more important things – we now had a staff room – Spartan enough but at least a staff room – and a cup of tea during the morning break.

In 1963, when I came to teach in St. Mary's, we worked a 32-hour classroom week (never a free class) with a 'half-day' Wednesday (3 p.m.) and Saturday 12.30 p.m. as well as long hours of preparation and correction. We stood at the corridor window during the morning break because there was nowhere else we could stand. There was no question of privacy, or even a place to sit. Those were the days when there were still tenants on the ground floor and space was at a premium. Facilities were meagre. There was no laboratory. I remember the science teacher doing marvels with a few weights and pieces of string, a couple of batteries and some lenses which she carried about with her from room to room. To me the significant thing was that the subject was being taught. In my previous school there was a perfectly good laboratory- but no teaching of science.

Working conditions then and to the last were never less than austere. When the gales blew, the top storey rocked and the building hummed loudly like a spinning top. It hummed and vibrated so loudly that it was impossible to hear or be heard. Teachers and pupils huddling in overcoats, peered at each other through the gathering gloom, while the building swayed and groaned, wind plucked at back and feet and heads and slates as big as the average table top hurtled past the window. Small wonder that teachers came and went with alarming regularity. For most it was a traumatic experience for which their higher diploma course did nothing to prepare them.

I had come south from a cosy little religious day school in Patrick Kavanagh country near the Border – coal fire in every room, civilised conversation over a cup of tea during the break, same type of pupil, same background. Boys cycled in from Kingscourt and Essexford or ambled down from the housing estates and small shops, just as they walked from Assumption place or cycled from Reenascreena and Barryroe to St. Mary's. One of my big surprises, on arrival was the different response in the classroom. Where northern boys were dour, incommunicative and spoke in monosyllables – though their written work was comprehensive enough – St. Mary's boys were voluble, affable, eager to talk, to question and to argue. There was a brightness and surface glitter about them that was completely lacking in the northern counterparts, whose minds, like icebergs, bulked large and moved secretly beneath the surface. It was as if St. Mary's boys were determined to present themselves in the most favourable light and were conscious of the need to do so at all times, whereas the northern boys seemed bent on parading themselves as inarticulate morons – something they were far from being. Both groups fared equally well in exams. It was in verbal communications that St. Mary's excelled.

Another marked difference between the two groups – and one which aroused my admiration from the beginning – was the difference in attitude towards jobs, which in the early sixties were hard enough to find. I had come from a school where half of any Leaving Cert. Class – after a few feeble efforts to find employment at home – rushed towards the emigrant boat. One of the most gratifying things about St. Mary's was that boys were oriented towards jobs at home. They were not too proud to take up temporary jobs – menial jobs if necessary – while they looked around for openings. Usually they were successful. Another cheering thing was the urge towards third-level education. Boys of quite average ability – but admirable determination – while engaged in temporary work were prepared to take grinds, attend evening classes, do whatever was necessary to get them into third-level institution on which they had set their sights.

A few years ago, I stood in the foyer of the Abbey Theatre in Dublin, where four boys from St. Mary's had just won the final of the Educational Building Society debating competition for Irish schools, and heard a well-known journalist, who was there to record the event for the Evening Herald, exclaim, as he walked away in some bemusement to file his report; 'Extraordinary school! Lay secondary for boys – woman Principal – never knew we had such places. Lads with minds sharp as razors- bloody marvellous!'

St. Mary's had its triumphs, its scholarship boys, its brilliant students who went out to grace the universities, the professions and the world of business. But, nowadays, when I sit at the Past Pupils' Annual Dinner and I hear the scholars and the prize-winners eulogized, I think of all those unsung heroes, the average boys, undistinguished academically, decent, honest, hardworking, conscientious, who passed through the school. It is boys like these I particularly cherish, boys who went on to become good husbands and fathers, responsible citizens, pillars of their own local community. I like to think they have brought with them something from St. Mary's, an openness to the world around them, and independence of mind, an ability to think for themselves, to sift through to the core of a matter, to express themselves cogently without fear or favour. This, rather than narrow academic achievement, I would hope, is the legacy of St. Mary's to the community. I have no regrets at the passing of St. Mary's. It served its purpose and it served it well. I would be the first to concede that there were many ways in which it might have served even better.

## Part II
*Speech at unveiling of the plaque 24 September 1993.*

When I met Mrs Dineen today, I told her I wasn't going to say a word. I will always remember the day she said to me, *'But you are only an employee'*.

I came here in 1963 and there were some unwritten rules to be observed. One was you never, never, never got sick. Mrs, Dineen didn't get sick therefore her teachers didn't get sick. She told that if she ever got a cold or a touch of the flu, she went to bed in the evenings with a bundle of Irish compositions; it's remarkable the cure that was in those Irish compositions, where Mrs Dineen was concerned and which did not seem to work for the rest of us. If you did get a cold or a touch of the flu and decided to stay at home, you went through a certain procedure. You rang up Mrs Dineen to say, 'I'm sick'. On noting the astonishment in her voice that you were well able to phone, you learned that it was better to let your wife ring the next time. When she did, Mrs Dineen would ask her two questions: 'Is he in bed?' and 'Has he had the doctor?' And if the answer was 'no' to both of these, well, you were considered the worst kind of malingerer.

The second rule was that you were never, ever again to take time off to go to the funerals of a friend or neighbour. Your friends and neighbours were expected to have the common decency to so arrange their departure that the funeral would be at the weekend. The third unwritten rule was that if you yourself thought of departing this life you would have to arrange your visit with Saint Peter for sometime during the summer holidays or certainly not before a suitable replacement was found.

Now, Ladies and Gentlemen, I'm here tonight to honour Mrs Dineen. I was very proud to work with Mrs Dineen. Anybody who met Mrs Dineen knew that she was totally dedicated to her job. I never remember Mrs Dineen, in the seventeen years I was in St. Mary's, ever missing a day. I can't remember anyway. All the rest of us did as any normal human being would do but Mrs Dineen – never. She was a woman who was held in great affection and with a certain degree of awe by all who knew her.

## Part III
*Condolences from Eamonn McGrath, 15 January, 1999.*

Please accept the condolences of Joan and myself, on the sad occasion of your mother's death. She was in poor health, I know, for the past few years and had reached a good age. Nevertheless the suddenness of her going is disconcerting.

I came to Clonakilty in 1963, at your mother's invitation, and from then until her school closed in 1980, was a member of her staff. During all that time, I found her a very direct and honest person, to deal with. She never asked anything of her teachers that she was not willing to do herself. I would be the first to acknowledge, that she was not well served by many of them.

What I valued, in particular, about her, was her directness and her honesty. We had many arguments, sharp enough at times, about school matters, but always she was able to transcend differences. When we met again, she behaved as if nothing had happened. Every day was a new beginning for her. That was a great quality. I can't recall, ever, meeting anyone else, who had it to such a degree. She was, also, a person of her word, something rare enough in life. I think that some of her teachers were too inexperienced, to understand or appreciate that.

She liked conflict, and functioned best in that kind of milieu. In what was essentially a man's world, she had the measure of most men. Anyone, who doubted the equality of the sexes, would have had to re-examine his prejudices, after a bruising encounter with her. I always respected her greatly for that. She did not suffer fools easily, and met quite a few in her time.

Her pupils knew her worth. For so many of them, she acted as a Guidance Teacher, before the term was invented. Many are grateful, to her today, because of her help. Her name will live on and wherever education in Clonakilty is the subject of discussion, she will have an honourable place. Incidentally, I was glad to see that her old school was, recently, re-roofed and is to be preserved for posterity, ideally, as a museum, built around her personality.

Hers was no easy life. Her family can only be grateful to her for the way she looked after them and saw to their education. Her pride in their achievements, was only matched be her attachment to her grandchildren, about whose educational prowess, she was in the habit of telling me, whenever we met.

She had a serene and happy retirement, and was as sharp-witted in her old age, as she ever was in her teaching years. Again, Traolach, I would like to offer the sympathy of Joan and myself to you and to every member of the family, on your great loss. I hope it may be some solace to you all, to know that your mother has become, for all time, part of the folklore of Clonakilty. I feel privileged to have known and worked with her.

# Appendix 2
# Jerry Beechinor R.I.P (pupil 1938–1942)

**Part I**

*Extract from talk given at unveiling of commemorative plaque*

I happen to be one of the students who took up here in 1938 when Ms Connaughton and her late husband opened their doors. I feel the least worthy of all the pupils, over the years, to have the honour to perform this function tonight but I am pleased to do this and proud to do it.

This occasion marks the 55th anniversary of the arrival in Clonakilty of Jeremiah J. Dineen and Ms Connaughton, who opened their secondary school here at this spot. I'm sure many of you remember, at least those of you who were here then.

I recall that time very well. They were difficult times, less affluent times. Our two teachers impressed us; they worked so hard and so fervently and in a caring way. We did benefit subsequently from the point of view of their caring attitude and their degree of discipline. The achievements of past students from 1938 to 1980 would bear testimony, I think, to the quality of education imparted. The people of Clonakilty and its hinterland owe a debt of gratitude to Mrs Dineen and her late husband. These two people were pioneers of secondary education in this part of West Cork. This was to be the foundation for a first-class, second-level college, in due course. They put dedication into teaching. They instilled into us pupils how to become more mature, more cultured and they taught us how to take our place in society. The fruit of their efforts can be seen in the number of former students who have distinguished themselves in flourishing careers, in business, including farming, in the academic world and in those who have left all to join the ministry of preachers.

Those of us who were fortunate enough to take up secondary

education here in 1938 recall that conditions were bad at that time. Many boys, here in West Cork were given the chance of competing for those things for which secondary education is essential. Before 1938, boys just did not have this opportunity but Mrs Dineen and her late husband put that right. There was no free secondary education either in 1938 or for many years afterwards: yet the two Dineens, Jeremiah and Margaret decided to take a risk in establishing a facility in the town. They were aware of the need and of course, they must have realised the challenges would not be little. However, they were undaunted and they had the qualifications and the ability for the task. Above all they had a vocation to teach. First, they bought their own premises and they gave of their best to the students in a generous and courageous spirit. With those of us who studied in the early years, we were very fortunate, including myself, in that the Principal, Mr Dineen had done a course of study in Dairy Science at UCC and he put his advice and encouragement at our service.

The history of St. Mary's was written in a little booklet published in 1980, but I believe the real history of St. Mary's is written in the lives and hearts of all of us who have been associated with St. Mary's. The gratitude and affection which all the students still have for St. Mary's, its Principal, Mrs Dineen and the teachers gave birth to the idea that we erect a plaque in the very place where the founders started. It is the clear wish of all of us that we perpetuate the memory of Jeremiah and Margaret Dineen and that we also recall the year that St. Mary's started when they gave the benefits of secondary education to us in Clonakilty from 1938.

On behalf of all past pupils, I unveil this plaque and I wish Mrs Dineen many years of happiness in retirement. Finally, I would like to thank my colleagues and committee for their advice and assistance and without which I would not be here tonight.

## Part II

*Concluding talk at unveiling of plaque.*

I will conclude now. From listening to everybody today, I wish to give just one message, which, to my mind, sums up Mrs Dineen. At school we learned the four cardinal virtues: prudence, temperance, fortitude and justice.

She is older than me but I have a lot of grey hairs myself now and I think the older you get the more one's age levels out so we are more on a level now. I have thought a lot about her ever since I left school and here tonight we have put together a picture focusing on Mrs Dineen. And the good example she is to so many of us is a tribute to her. She is a perfect example of a lay person in today's world who carried these virtues in exemplary fashion. She has blazed a trail in a truly Christian way, in true faith. We are saying to her: *"Mrs Dineen, this is your life as we see it."* Of course, it is only a minute section of your life but we have crystallised here as best we could your life, focusing on the major points and we thank you very much.

## Part III

*Extract from Homily preached by Fr. Jim Duggan CSSp at the concelebrated Mass prior to the unveiling of the plaque.*

I refer to that time in the late thirties and early forties. I chose the Gospel of the Good Samaritan because of the kind, caring and loving person that Samaritan turned out to be and I compare it to the caring, loving and sympathetic attitude extended to us in St. Mary's. Jeremiah and Margaret Dineen extended that care to each and every one of us. We owe a debt of gratitude to both of them for their care and interest in each and every one of us and for what we have achieved in life. Certainly, after God and our parents we owe this to teachers in our schools. Certainly, St. Mary's has contributed to the well-being of us all through the years. The Dineens were the good Samaritans for all of us.

The actual length of years is not that important, whether it be silver, golden or diamond jubilees; rather it is the depth and breadth of the achievement of any person or any institution which is important. Now the depth and the breadth of achievement in St. Mary's College, begun by Mr and Mrs Dineen and assisted by the various teachers is something we thank God for. I wish to mention the depth of knowledge, the intuition and guidance and the help that were given to the students, helping them to achieve good results. Certainly, they gave of their best to assist each and every one of us with that caring and loving attitude which they extended to all of us. We are grateful to God for all you did and we pray God to bless you and your family and the teachers and indeed all the students who supported one another through the years. Those early years were not easy. They were the war years but they gave of their best. It was not easy to run a school at that particular time.

May the grace of God which was given to us in Baptism, to bring us to a greater love of God, continue to grow in us so that we may all be united one day in the great school of Heaven where knowledge and love will reach perfection and this for all eternity.

# Appendix 3

*Words by Pope John Paul II to teachers, 22 January, 1993.*

"Let your first concern therefore be to propose the fundamental human virtues on which the human being can be solidly built; prudence, justice, fortitude and temperance. 'The human virtues', states the Catechism of the Catholic Church, 'are firm attitudes, stable dispositions, habitual perfections of the intellect and will that govern our actions, direct our passions and guide our conduct according to reason and faith. They produce facility, self-control and joy in leading a morally good life. The virtuous person is one who freely does what is good."

# Saint Marys

We remember old Saint Marys
Many stories they are told
Of years of education
Of brave lads & of bold
And the winding hill we climbed each day
Beginning on life's path
With thoughts of Bean Uí Dhuinnín
God bless her golden heart.

And we started out on dreams then
That seemed so far away
And crossed the many bridges
That leads us to today
As we sing of alma mater
Whether near or far from home
And live again the memories of St. Marys.

Young men came from many miles
To learn her precious code
The Gaeilge, French & Latin
And histories of old
And when lads didn't meet up
To standards set on high
A little kind persuasion
Forced them into line.

We recall the handball alley
And the games we used to play
Where many scores were settled
At the end of every day

As we climbed the hill up in the field
That overlooks the town
We talked about horizons
And what would the future hold

Now men have strayed to foreign shores
And men have stayed at home
Some in search of fortune
And some out seeking souls
But a bond stands there uniting them
Across the land and sea
From roots grown in the memories of St. Marys

The days of black & amber
Still linger in our minds
And tours we made to other schools
When we sung our party rhymes
But the games that stand out best of all
And hold a place in time
Were those played round the walls of old St. Marys.

The early morning cigarette
The odd curse & the swear
The bubble gum & the races run
For leader down the stairs
And thoughts of fair young maidens
On a hill too far away
The Angelus as Ghaeilge
A part of daily prayer.

*Words, Music & Lyrics by ROB/ Ruaskin (1987)*
*O'Donovan Brothers, Ballyduvane*